BEST SELLER

AN EASY TO UNDERSTAND
OVERVIEW OF THE
BESTSELLING BOOK
OF ALL TIME

LAURIE DRIESEN

© 2025 Laurie Driesen

All rights reserved. No part of this book may be reproduced, stored in a retrieval system, or transmitted in any form or by any means, digital, electronic, mechanical, photocopying, recording, or otherwise, without prior written permission from the publisher.

Published by Silver Path Resources LLC

ISBN 978-0-9962030-2-9
ISBN 978-0-9962030-3-6 (pbk)

Cover Design by Thauer Art Direction
Divider Image by freepik.com
Interior Design by Crystal L Barnes, Better Way Publishing LLC, www.crystal-barnes.com

Scripture taken from The Holy Bible, New International Version. Copyright © 1973, 1978, 1984 International Bible Society. Used by permission of Zondervan Bible Publishers.

DEDICATION

Best Seller is dedicated to Kristin Falkner, who unknowingly inspired me to create an easy-to-understand overview of the Bible. We had been meeting regularly for years regarding business matters. She was not a Christian at the time and had never read the Bible. Through our conversations, I sensed that the Holy Spirit was working within her and she was seeking the one true God. Though typically I gave her business-related books for her birthday, I decided to give her a special gift for her birthday that year. I knew that when I gave her a wrapped book, she would assume it was another business book. To prepare her for the book that she would not be expecting, I wrote a one-page description called "Bestseller" to provide an overview of the book I hoped she would read.

As she held the wrapped gift in her hands, I read the overview aloud. She had no idea what book I was referring to until about halfway through the description. I'll always remember the look on her face when, after hearing about the power and magnitude of the bestselling book of all time, she realized she was holding the Bible, the precious Word of God. There were tears in her eyes and she was truly happy to become the owner of such an extraordinary book.

She immediately committed to reading the entire Bible from beginning to end. Thus began her journey of learning all she could from studying the Word of God. Her experience

DEDICATION

inspired me to write this book, an easy-to-understand overview of the Bible for people who don't know where the Bible came from, whether it's true, and what it's all about. The overview that I wrote for Kris became the introduction, the first reading you'll find in *Best Seller*.

ACKNOWLEDGEMENTS AND GRATITUDE

My sister, Linda Lijewski, for proofing and editing *Best Seller* and for her encouragement throughout this project.

Pastor and author Bruce Osborn for providing the theological review.

Kristin Falkner, for allowing me to share her journey of faith and study of God's Word.

CONTENTS

The Bestselling Book of All Time ix

Part 1: The Bible

    Chapter 1: In the Beginning 1

    Chapter 2: Where Did the Bible Come From? 9

    Chapter 3: What is in the Bible 15

    Chapter 4: Proof that the Bible is the Word of God 25

    Chapter 5: The Inspired Scriptures 41

    Chapter 6: The Law, Laws, and More Laws 51

    Chapter 7: Translations of the Bible 57

    Chapter 8: Price of the Bestselling Book 65

Part 2: The Themes of the Bible

    Chapter 9: Themes within the Bible 71

    Chapter 10: The Theme of the Covenants 75

    Chapter 11: God's Chosen People 83

    Chapter 12: Reconciliation with God 91

    Chapter 13: The Love of God 95

    Chapter 14: Reversal of Destiny 101

    Chapter 15: The Names of God 107

Contents

    Chapter 16: The Tabernacle, Temple, and Heaven ... 119

Part 3: The Power of the Bible

    Chapter 17: The Power of the Word of God 127

    Chapter 18: Sharper than a Two-edged Sword 139

    Chapter 19: Nourishment for Our Souls 145

    Chapter 20: The Depth of the Bible 149

    Chapter 21: Wisdom for Life 157

    Chapter 22: The Power to Save 167

    Chapter 23: The Power of God's Will Revealed 175

    Chapter 24: Power to Live the Christian Life 185

Part 4: The Star of the Bible

    Chapter 25: Who is the Star of the Bible? 193

    Chapter 26: The Shadow of Jesus 197

    Chapter 27: Everlasting Jesus 201

    Chapter 28: The Feasts Fulfilled 205

    Chapter 29: Why Did Jesus Come to Earth? 209

    Chapter 30: God Revealed Himself Through Jesus .. 213

    Chapter 31: The Revelation of Jesus Christ 223

Conclusion 231

Author's Note — What's Next? 236

Steps to Salvation 237

Bibliography 239

THE BESTSELLING BOOK OF ALL TIME

You may have a copy of this bestselling book right in your own home.

This book contains more wisdom than any other book on the market. It will give you knowledge about the Creator of the universe, God's plan of salvation, relationships, work, money, marriage, health, and much more.

This book will become your very best friend. It will be there when you are lonely. It will comfort you when you are grieving. It will give you hope when you can't see the end of the road. It will light your path when you don't know which way to turn. It will heal you when you are hurting. It will cut you open when you need to change. It will fill you up when you feel empty. It will make you cry. It will make you laugh. It will give you the greatest peace you've ever known. It will give you the greatest joy you've ever felt. It will make you feel complete.

The bestselling book is:
- ✛ A light that shows you the right path
- ✛ A fire that burns away your imperfections
- ✛ A hammer that breaks the hardest rock
- ✛ A sword that will cut your heart open
- ✛ Balm that will heal you
- ✛ Water that will wash you clean
- ✛ A refuge when you have no one else

✦ Food that satiates your hungry soul
✦ A sword when you are in a battle
✦ The plumb line of truth to expose lies

And so much more.

This book holds more variety than any other book. It offers you:

Mystery, history, romance, murder, poetry, royalty, kings, queens, wars, songs, love, friendship, countries being raised up, countries being torn down, stories of success, and stories of failure. It answers your deepest questions about the "whys" of life and the world. And if you want to know what will happen in the future, it even discloses what is to come.

It is the story of God's relationship with people, how He loves, how He helps, how He judges, how He saves, how He disciplines, how He makes things right, and that He is the all-powerful, all-knowing God of the entire universe.

Not only is this book a bestseller, it is the ***bestselling book of all time.***

Over 5 billion copies have been sold and distributed around the world, with 100 million still being sold every year. Portions of it have been translated into over 2,500 languages.

THIS IS NO ORDINARY BOOK.

It is a compilation of 66 books, written by 40 different authors over the course of 1,500 years. The authors include a farmer, tax collector, tentmaker, doctor, fishermen, shepherds, kings, priests, government officials, and prophets. The books include prophecies that have been fulfilled and miracles that have been documented. Eyewitnesses who walked with Jesus carefully recorded what they saw and heard so that we could come to know the Savior. All the authors wrote by the inspiration of the Holy Spirit. Therefore, there is only one Author of this book.

The documents contained in this book were diligently examined for many years by councils and church leaders. Numerous other writings were discarded for lack of evidence or proof of validity. The books included in the final copy stood the test of truth, authority, doctrine, and inspiration. The result: **God's Word**. His revelation. His message, left on this earth for all of us, including you and me.

Take this book and hold it in your hands. The book you hold has withstood scrutiny, criticism, threats, and vicious attacks. Translators were persecuted and martyred so that you and I could read this book in our own language. Over the centuries, millions have been put to death because they believed what this book says. It has been and still is forbidden in many countries to own this book. If authorities in some countries found this book in your home, you would be imprisoned or killed. Most of the writers of this book paid the highest price—their own blood—to boldly proclaim their faith, their story, the words on the pages that you and I read today.

The bestseller that you are holding in your hands is more valuable than silver, gold, and worldly wealth. That means it's priceless. The Author of the bestselling book of all time is **God**.

It is…

The Bible

PART 1

The Bible

CHAPTER 1

In the Beginning

The very first sentence of the Bible says,

> *"In the beginning God created the heavens and the earth." (Genesis 1:1)*

"In the beginning God…"

This is a huge statement! God? How do we know there's a God? And for the first sentence of the Bible to boldly state that God created the heavens and the earth, what's the proof? There were no witnesses, at least no human witnesses, and no corroborating records. How can we be sure that the very first sentence of the Bible is true?

HOW DID THE WORLD COME TO BE?

When you look at a beautiful work of art or a towering skyscraper, have you ever asked yourself, "I wonder how that came to be?" Probably not. Inherently you know that if there is a work of art, there must have been an artist who created it. If a skyscraper is towering over you, it was planned by architects and built by construction workers. We know by common sense and reason that paint and bricks aren't thrown up in the air, only to fall down precisely into place, becoming an orderly and beautiful handiwork.

Part 1: The Bible

Through the work of art or the construction of a building, we learn things about the person who created it. The result, the finished product, reveals something about the artist, composer, architect, builder, producer, or inventor. We can actually learn, to some extent, about the person and personality behind the creation.

So it is with this bold, matter-of-fact statement that begins the Bible. **God created the heavens and the earth.** We know this is true. We know that nature didn't happen by accident; we know that there weren't objects flying through empty space that just happened to come together magically to form complex, orderly systems in the heavens and earth. Instinctively we recognize that there is a higher, supreme being that is powerful and knowledgeable enough to create things that are beyond our comprehension. The heavens and earth keep us reaching, studying, and learning, although its vastness and magnitude are far beyond our ability to grasp.

Some people try to tell us that it was an accident, a big explosion, or billions of years of development to bring the heavens and earth to the point of full systems of orderliness, function, and beauty. Their "faith" is a supposition that something complex and orderly developed out of chaos. It is a guess, a theory that has no precedent or proof. Has anything that exploded ever rained down its chaotic mess of fragments to the ground into an orderly structure or become warm-blooded bodies that live and breathe?

With their assumption and presumption, they claim that atoms formed the sun, moon, planets, and earth. Oceans appeared, cells formed and became more complex, then progressed to become live animals, which evolved into complex, feeling, thoughtful, innovative, unique human beings.

My response to them is a simple one. "It takes more faith to believe that all that exists came to be by accident or evolution than to believe that there is a God who created the heavens and the earth."

WE CAN BE SURE IT'S TRUE

How can we be so sure that the first sentence of the Bible is true? We have assurance because the result of Genesis 1:1 is right in front of us. The world that God created in the beginning is still flourishing right before our very eyes every day. The rhythm, beauty, and power of nature is a constant testimony and reminder of God. The sun rises and sets every day. The seasons come and pass in their prescribed times. The rain falls and accomplishes its assignment to water the earth. The oceans obey their boundaries; the species of animals follow their roles in creation.

Nature is God's physical, constant testimony to everyone around the world. It is one way He reveals Himself to people. Even those who have never heard about God engage with His creation every day. The sun rises and sets everywhere on earth and speaks in the same language to all people. No corner of earth is missed and the wondrous voice of creation testifies that there is a God. All people everywhere are exposed to the same witness, the same proof, in the same visual language, with no barriers.

Not only does such a constant testimony prove that God exists, but the Bible tells us in Psalm 19:1,

> "The heavens declare the glory of God; the skies proclaim the work of his hands."

In fact, the heavens and earth and all of creation actually

reveal attributes of God and His personality.

God's power. Billions of galaxies. The heights of the mountains. The heat of the sun. The depths of the oceans. The millions of insects, fish, and animals. The winds of the atmosphere. The microscopic atoms. The very breath in our lungs that keeps us alive. God's power is awesome and incomprehensible. How much power does it take to keep that huge ball of the sun burning? There is so much to learn about the immensity of God's creation.

God's provision. God is personally involved in His creation. The Bible tells us that God shows His kindness through His provision in nature. Acts 14:17 tells us,

> *"Yet he has not left himself without testimony: He has shown kindness by giving you rain from heaven and crops in their seasons; he provides you with plenty of food and fills your hearts with joy."*

When we think of everything we need to exist on this planet, God has graciously provided it to us. The sun sustains life on earth. The moon provides the pull of gravity that stabilizes the earth. The mixture of gases in the atmosphere provides the air we breathe. The oceans provide necessary water for our lives. The earth provides for the food chain. God designed His creation to provide for our needs.

God's creativity. The creativity of God cannot be explained in just a few sentences. The beauty, majesty, and variety in His creation cause us to be in awe of Him. Just look at mountains, canyons, forests, waterfalls, rainbows, fish, birds, and the wide variety of animals. Virtually every color is displayed in the landscape, plants, and flowers. A friend started learning how to paint. As she was painting a tree, she realized that she never knew how many shades of green there are in the color palette of nature. A tree is not just green leaves and a brown trunk. There are many hues that make up the intricacies of colors in just the leaves alone.

Clearly, God is not only creative, but in some ways, He has a sense of humor that is displayed by some of His animals (and insects). When my husband and I watch nature programs, we laugh and comment about God's sense of humor as we watch birds dance, monkeys swing from tree to tree, and colorful fish with funny faces swim in the depth of the ocean. God is amazingly creative!

God's faithfulness. The simple fact that the sun always rises in the east and sets in the west is a testimony to God's faithfulness. We never worry about whether the sun will actually rise the next day. We know that it will because it always has. The sunrise is faithful, steadfast, and continuous. Could it be that our God, the Creator, the One who designed the pattern of daily sunrises and sunsets, is just as faithful as His creation demonstrates? We have a daily testimony, first thing every morning, that the Creator is alive and well, personally involved with His creation, and testifying in a loud visual voice, "I am faithful!"

God's love. The Bible tells us in Genesis 1:27 that God created man in His own image. Mankind is the part of God's creation that truly expresses the love of God. Every person has his or her own particular DNA, which is unique from every other person on earth. The Bible tells us of God's love, but the fact that He created each of us with our own DNA and fingerprint is a physical reminder that we are not cookie cutter, unimportant human beings. We are unique individuals, created in God's image, with our own exclusive physical characteristics.

IS NATURE THE ONLY PROOF THAT GOD EXISTS?

Nature alone is not adequate to personally know God, but nature gives us a foundation of assurance that God exists, He is real, and He is good. Nature is a daily, constant witness to the glory, majesty, and power of God. No one can say, "I had no idea there is a God."

God is not in nature or a part of nature. He is not in a tree or a blade of grass, as some belief systems may claim. God is the artist and the heavens and earth are His creation. They are to be admired and enjoyed but not worshipped. This is very important. Some believe that God is "in everything," that is to say, in every tree, plant, animal, and person. This is not Biblical. God does not dwell or inhabit each piece of His creation any more than an artist actually indwells the piece of art he has painted.

The only part of God's creation that is blessed with the indwelling of God Himself is each man or woman who is made alive in Christ through faith.

THOSE WHO DENY GOD

The Bible admonishes and condemns people who look at nature, the sunrise, the sunset, the majesty of mountains, the intricacy of creation, and still claim there is no God. Psalm 14:1a says,

> *"The fool says in his heart, 'There is no God.'"*

Furthermore, God's wrath will be poured out on people who suppress the truth that is plainly revealed to them. Romans 1:18-20 says,

> *"The wrath of God is being revealed from heaven against all the godlessness and wickedness of men who suppress the truth by their wickedness, since what may be known about God is plain to them, because God has made it plain to them. For since the creation of the world God's invisible qualities—his eternal power and divine nature—have been clearly seen, being understood from what has been made, so that men are without excuse."*

If you ever talk with someone who claims to have never heard of God or Jesus or the Gospel message, you can ask the person, "What do you think of nature? The Creator? Tell me your thoughts about the majesty of God's creation."

The answer to that question will reveal the heart of the person. Awe and praise of a supreme Creator? Or rebellion against God and the foolish supposition that the most intricate and beautiful work of art came about by accident or billions of years of evolution? An intelligent design is evidence of an intelligent designer.

IN THE BEGINNING... GOD

The credibility of the Bible rests on this first sentence, this important claim that is boldly stated as you open the pages of Scripture. If you don't believe that God created all things, you will wobble and waver in your ability to believe the rest of the powerful Word of God. If you trust and believe that the first sentence of the Bible is true, you have a firm foundation to continue reading, learning, and understanding the mind of God and Scriptural truth.

Do you believe that God created the heavens and the earth?

CHAPTER 2

Where Did the Bible Come From?

When we open the pages of Scripture, beginning with Genesis, we find ourselves reading about historical events and stories of the lives of ancient Hebrew people. Some may wonder if the records of these events are true and why the personal lives of the Hebrew people are in the Bible. We are reading the archives, the documented history of lives and events that were carefully recorded by the ancient Hebrews.

The sacred writings of the Hebrew Bible (the Tanakh) were comprised of their history, records, prophecies, genealogies, life stories, psalms, and other writings that were carefully (and miraculously) preserved by the Hebrew people. The Old Testament of our Christian Bible consists of many of the writings of the Hebrew Bible.

These Hebrew documents are included in the Christian Bible for Believers in Jesus to fully understand Christianity. Christ is foreshadowed in many of the Hebrew writings. Jesus is the long-awaited Messiah that was foretold in the prophecies of the Hebrew sacred texts. The Old Testament provides a foundational understanding of God, the history of His interaction with His people, the Law (God's standards of behavior), and prophecies of the coming Messiah.

The New Testament was written over 400 years after the

last writing of the Old Testament. The New Testament focuses on the Savior, the Messiah who fulfilled what the Old Testament foretold. Eyewitness accounts of Jesus as well as letters or "epistles" were written to the various churches that organized after His resurrection. These are the documents that make up the New Testament we have today. The New Testament also includes a record of the Apostles and how the church was formed. The last book of the Bible is a prophetic book about the end times of our world written by the Apostle John who received revelations directly from the Lord Jesus. And so, we have the complete message, the Old Testament and the New Testament, in one book that you and I can read, study, and learn about God.

When we read the Bible from Genesis to Revelation, we learn the whole story from creation to the end times of the world. And the story consists of 66 individual books, written by 40 different authors, over the course of 1,500 years, and in three continents (Asia, Africa and Europe). Wow! What began as thousands of writings, records, and documents became consolidated, verified, and carefully compiled into one precious, Holy Book.

How did the Bible begin?

Before the Jewish people wrote and documented the records of events, the history of their people was taught and learned orally. The ancient Jewish people believed very strongly in passing the stories of their people down to the next generation. They memorized the events of their history and passed them along orally to their families.

As the Jews relayed their history orally to their children, they weren't just sharing embellished, short stories, told in the way they felt the best telling them. No, they were memorized accurately and specifically, and they ensured that what they recounted was told exactly the same way every time. Their history was very important to them and it was crucial to make sure that all details were consistent and correct.

Although the ancient Hebrew people relied on their oral tradition of passing their history on to the next generation, there came a point in time when they began recording the history of the events in writing. Some of their writings have been in existence since 1,400 years before Christ and eventually became part of the Bible.

Some might be tempted to believe that people in ancient times changed their history, made mistakes in copying texts, or messed up their records. After all, they didn't have computers or files or the methods of organization that we have today. If you believe that the ancient Jewish people didn't keep good records, you would be wrong. What they did to preserve their records and written documents was extremely powerful and unique. They had scribes that were dedicated to accurately copying scrolls and documents. Their methods of copying every single letter were careful, accurate, and precise.

WHO PUT THE BIBLE TOGETHER?

After Jesus ascended to Heaven and the church was growing, many documents and records were written. It is believed that the original New Testament documents were written during the span of about 50 years beginning about 20 years after Jesus was resurrected. Letters and writings were copied and circulated to the churches in Asia Minor, Rome, Corinth, and Macedonia. Over time, there were thousands of copies of many documents spreading throughout those areas of the world. Parts of what we read today in our Bible were actually being circulated and read by many people for decades before the writings were more formally compiled.

As Christianity spread and churches grew, church leaders began to realize that it was necessary to sift through the writings, identify authentic documents, and compile one core book. Considering that the books of the Bible were written over the course of over 1,500 years by 40 different authors, can you imagine the complexity of putting these writings together into one single book?

Yet one book was needed. One single book out of the massive amount of text, documents, and writings that were in existence. One Holy Book that would hold only the writings that were authoritative and inspired by the Holy Spirit. God's message to mankind, His Word, His love letter to the world… in one unique book.

Over the course of hundreds of years, various councils and church leaders evaluated the massive amount of information and documents. They began this process several hundred years after the resurrection of Jesus. They intended to compile the valid, inspired, authoritative documents into one book. This book would be the core, the one group of documents that would be the pure, Holy Word of God, without being mixed with the many other writings that were being circulated at the time.

This book would be the true, Holy Bible that had been validated by church leaders. This would be the "canon" of Scripture. The word "canon" is defined as, "an accepted principle or rule" or "a criterion or standard of judgment" or "a body of principles, rules, standards, or norms."[1]

Where Did the Bible Come From?

THE CANON OF SCRIPTURE

Councils, church leaders, and popes met and made decisions about which documents should be compiled into one book. There was much discussion among church leaders and scholars as to the authority and credibility of the writings during the early years of the Church. They had lists of books including the Gospel accounts and the epistles. There were many other books and writings that were not considered to be inspired and therefore were not included in the final canon. They may have been written anonymously or were not able to be verified as authoritative.

It is this point that critics of the Bible focus on to argue and disprove the authority of Scripture. They consider that when fallible people are involved in such a holy process, it can't be trusted. That is a false assumption and reflects a lack of knowledge and understanding of the process of how the canon of Scripture was decided. It also demonstrates a lack of faith in the power of God Almighty to control His very own message to us. The truth is that God chose to use human beings as the tools and the conduit through which He would disseminate His words and message to mankind.

Our amazing God used human beings, empowered by the Holy Spirit, to go through the process of determining which books would make up the canon of Scripture. The Holy Spirit would powerfully work through the people involved, and the final precious copy of the Bible would be proven, tested, and meet the standards of inspiration and authority.

Among the criteria for the books to be included in the canon of Scripture were:

+ *Authorship* – The book was written by an Apostle or someone who walked closely with a Disciple or

Apostle.
- + *Inspiration* – The book was inspired by the Holy Spirit, in other words, given by revelation of God.
- + *Theological consistency* – The theology of the book was consistent with other accepted Christian documents.

There were also other criteria that were evaluated and required, such as historical accuracy, fulfillment of certain prophecies, and acceptance of the book by early church leaders. The criteria for verifying the authority and validity of the writings were taken very seriously. The process was a serious and holy endeavor that took hundreds of years until the canonization of Scripture was affirmed by councils and church leaders.

The result was the Holy Scriptures without the cumbersome amount of writings that did not meet the standard to be included. The book we hold in our hands is the final copy, the true revelation, the words that God inspired through human writers. God working through people, as He loves to do!

CHAPTER 3

What is in the Bible

If you have read the Bible from beginning to end, you have probably noticed that the books are not in chronological order. The Bible is a collection of writings that is organized by sections and categories.

The Christian Bible has two sections, the Old Testament and the New Testament. The Old Testament contains the Law of God, which explains the standard of behavior God expects from His people, as well as prophecies, historical records, and books of wisdom of the Jewish people.

The New Testament testifies to the life of Jesus Christ, the birth of the Christian church, letters to the churches, and the revelation of what is to come in the future.

In very simple terms, the Old Testament teaches us about the expectations of God and reveals where we fall short. After all, we wouldn't know what sin is if not for the Law that defines for us what is right and wrong. The New Testament teaches us about the New Covenant of Grace which is the Gospel of Jesus Christ. The New Covenant (New Testament) is the answer to the problem of sin and man's inability to keep the Law of God.

Part 1: The Bible

THE OLD TESTAMENT

Among many types of writings in the Old Testament, you will read amazing stories and miracles that may be familiar to you. David and Goliath, Noah's Ark, Daniel in the Lion's Den, and the Parting of the Red Sea are found in the Old Testament. The 23rd Psalm, the wisdom of the Proverbs, and Isaiah's prophetic words that are told in the Christmas story are all found in the Old Testament.

The Old Testament consists of 39 books (written in Hebrew and some in Aramaic) which are generally broken down into four categories:
1. **The Law**
2. **History**
3. **Wisdom**
4. **Prophecy**

Here is a brief overview of what is contained in each of these categories.

THE LAW

The first five books of the Hebrew Bible comprise the Torah, which is the Law and is also known as the Pentateuch in the Christian Bible. Genesis, the first book of the Law, describes the beginning of the world, the first people that God created, and Abraham, the man chosen by God to become the patriarch of the nation of Israel. There are several other individuals whose lives are highlighted in Genesis. Abraham's son, Isaac, was miraculously born to Abraham and Sarah in their old age. Isaac's son, Jacob, had 12 sons that became the heads of the 12 tribes of Israel. These tribes formed the nation of Israel and for centuries the people traced their genealogies back to the tribe of their lineage. Jacob's son, Joseph, is another individual whose story is told in Genesis and whose life significantly impacted the nation of Israel.

As we read the next book of the Law, Exodus, we learn about the eventual slavery of the Hebrew people in Egypt. They were enslaved for 400 years, then God called Moses to lead the people out of bondage and into freedom. The parting of the Red Sea was one of the first legs of their journey through the wilderness to the land that God had promised to the people. The Ten Commandments were given by God to Moses at that time.

The remainder of the five books of the Law cover God's expectations of His people, the laws that God gave to the people, and a record of their history. After 400 years of slavery, they needed to learn a whole new way of life and God provided instruction through His Law. When we read about God's laws, we learn what matters to God and how He expected His people to obey, worship, and interact with Him.

THE HISTORY

The history of the Hebrew people is fascinating. The books of History include Joshua, Judges, Ruth, 1 & 2 Samuel, 1 & 2 Kings, 1 & 2 Chronicles, Ezra, Nehemiah, and Esther. We learn about the first three kings of Israel: King Saul, King David, and King Solomon. After King Solomon's reign, Israel split into two nations. Records of the kings of both Israel and Judah are in this section of the Old Testament. Many kings were evil and rebellious and some were faithful to God. As we read through the problems and the sins of the people, we learn more about God's love and faithfulness.

This section of the Bible also describes specific events in the lives of certain individuals because their actions impacted the nation and their life experiences teach us about God. We learn of David, who was a "man after God's own heart." He defended God's name during the war between Israel and the Philistine army. With a slingshot he killed the Philistine giant named Goliath in a one-to-one battle for victory of the war. David became the second king of Israel.

It is exciting to read about the miracles that God performed for individuals and for the nation of Israel. Study of these historical books strengthens our faith as we witness the reality of God in these true stories.

THE BOOKS OF WISDOM

The books that fall in the Wisdom category are the books of Job, Psalms, Proverbs, Ecclesiastes, and Song of Solomon. The book of Job tells us about a powerful, wealthy man who lost everything, including his children, all in one day. God's responses to Job's questions about why he was suffering are recorded in this book. The book of Job exposes the problem of suffering and reveals a sovereign, loving God that we can trust in all circumstances.

The book of Psalms is the song book or hymn book of the Jewish people. The Psalms minister to us as we learn to pour our hearts out to the Lord and to praise Him in the midst of any circumstance. The Psalms are a collection of writings, pleas for God to help in times of trouble, and songs and poems of praises to God.

The book of Proverbs contains sayings and statements of wisdom that, although written in ancient times, are still applicable to us today. "Wise men store up knowledge, but the mouth of the fool invites ruin." (Proverbs 10:14) King Solomon, the wisest man who ever lived, wrote these powerful life principles that guide us as we seek wisdom. Solomon also wrote Ecclesiastes and Song of Solomon. Ecclesiastes is his narrative of trying to seek happiness in the world and the realization that following God and seeking His will are the only way to be fulfilled.

THE BOOKS OF PROPHECY

The books of Prophecy consist of Isaiah all the way through Malachi, the end of the Old Testament. The Major Prophets are Isaiah, Jeremiah, Lamentations, Ezekiel, and Daniel. The rest of the prophetic books are considered the Minor Prophets because they are shorter in length. These books contain the prophecies of God concerning the nation of Israel. As you read through the Bible, don't skip these books! You would miss hearing God's voice throughout many pages of Scripture. You will actually get to know God better by reading His very words, spoken through the prophets, written in these books of prophecy.

There were many prophets in ancient Biblical times. This was one of the ways God spoke to His people. A prophet is one who speaks for the Lord and proclaims what God has instructed the person to say.

The book of Isaiah warns the people of sin and judgment and foretells the coming of the Messiah. The book of Jeremiah also warns of God's judgment and hope for the future. Both of these books have many passages that contain promises and encouragement for us to praise the Lord.

Have you heard the story of the prophet Jonah who was swallowed by a large fish? You'll find the amazing details of this event and the repentance of the city of Ninevah in the book of Jonah.

Part 1: The Bible

Daniel is a very important book that tells us about Daniel's life in captivity in Babylon. The miracle of Daniel in the Lion's Den is described in this book. The book of Daniel is also a very important book of prophecies about Jesus and the end times of the world.

The book of Hosea draws us into the life of Hosea the prophet who married a prostitute. God instructed the prophet to marry an unfaithful woman so that Hosea's very life would be a picture of God's steadfast love and faithfulness to the unfaithful nation that committed spiritual adultery against God.

In the books of Prophecy, we read the predictions, instructions, and the very words of God spoken through the prophets. Many times you'll read, "Thus says the Lord..." or "The mouth of the Lord has spoken...." These are direct quotes from God Himself. It is exciting, terrifying, and fulfilling to hear what God says from His own mouth!

The books of Prophecy help us to know God's heart and learn to trust Him. Much of prophecy may be hard to understand but some passages are very clear. It helps to refer to a Bible commentary so that you can look up the passages for an explanation and a deeper understanding.

Some may be thinking, "Sounds great but (yawn) I'm not really that interested in the stories and history of the ancient Hebrew people. What does that have to do with me?"

Years ago, when going through a very hard time in my life, I attended a Bible Study that focused on the Minor Prophets in the Old Testament. I remember thinking, *I don't want to study the Old Testament, I need help! How can the Minor Prophets help me?* I was not interested in reading the Old Testament. However, I stayed with the study and, to my surprise, very quickly fell in love with the Old Testament. It was amazing to study about God's people, how God helped them, and the events that the Jewish people went through. I began to understand that learning about God's relationship with His people teaches me about God, His ways, His personality, what's important to Him, and most of all, His great love. I got to know God better. My relationship with Him grew tremendously by learning how He responds, the miracles He performed, and the blessings He poured out on His people.

Through the writings and books of the Old Testament, we come to know what bothers God, what makes Him angry, and what He expects from the people He created. When we read about the failures of His people, we see ourselves in their actions. The Bible is like a mirror that reflects back to us insights about our very selves. Human nature has not changed over the centuries. We see our shortcomings and we learn the consequences of sin. We read about the patience of God, His heart that longs to bless His people, and His forgiveness that He so willingly extends to the humble and repentant.

The depth of what we learn about God in the Old Testament is fundamental to have an understanding of the God we worship.

THE NEW TESTAMENT

The New Testament contains 27 books (written in Greek) that fall into four categories:
1. **The Gospels**
2. **The Acts of the Apostles**
3. **The Epistles**
4. **The Book of Revelation**

Here is a brief overview of the categories found in the

PART 1: THE BIBLE

New Testament.

THE GOSPELS

The word gospel means "good message" or "good news." The Gospels are records of the life of Jesus, His miracles, teachings, crucifixion, and resurrection. These accounts are found in the books of Matthew, Mark, Luke, and John. In the Gospels you'll read about the miraculous birth of Jesus and the amazing events of His life. The Gospels include eyewitness accounts of the miracles of Jesus including healing the blind man, walking on the water, raising Lazarus from the dead, turning the water into wine, and more. The Gospels introduce us to twelve men that were called by Jesus to be His closest Disciples. Also included in the Gospel records are the crucifixion and the appearances of Jesus after His resurrection. Salvation is truly the good news of the Gospel message!

THE ACTS OF THE APOSTLES

The book of Acts describes the birth of the Christian church and the spread of Christianity. In this section of the New Testament, you'll read about the persecution of the Church led by a man named Saul. He relentlessly pursued Christians to arrest them and put them to death. He stood by watching as the first Christian martyr, Stephen, was being stoned to death. While Saul was on his way to Damascus to continue his deadly pursuit of Christians, Jesus appeared to him with a bright light. Saul fell off his horse, blinded by the flash of light. This event began Saul's conversion which can be found in Acts chapter 9. This is an amazing story of the conversion of a man who would become the greatest missionary the world has ever known.

Saul used his Roman name, Paul, as Jesus called him to preach among the Gentiles (non-Jewish people). Paul was powerfully used by the Lord to start the Christian church among the Gentiles and to clarify the doctrines of Christianity.

THE EPISTLES

The Epistles are correspondence by the Apostles to individuals and churches. These letters addressed needs of the churches and sometimes problems that had developed. The Epistles teach us about salvation, the Holy Spirit, Christian doctrine, how to live the Christian life, correction of specific activities in the churches, and warnings of false teachings.

THE BOOK OF REVELATION

Revelation is a prophetic book written by the Apostle John who wrote revelations that were given to him by Jesus. In some Bibles this book is titled "The Revelation of Jesus Christ" or "The Revelation to John." The book of Revelation begins with letters to seven churches, dictated by Jesus to the Apostle John. The rest of the book describes events that will take place in the end times, the second coming of Jesus, and the culmination of God's plan to be victorious over sin and evil.

GOD'S MESSAGE TO HUMANITY

The Bible can be described as God's message to mankind. It is an amazing adventure to delve into Scripture and learn about God's people, His great love for us, and the history of how Christianity began. The many denominations of Christianity base their system of beliefs on what the Bible teaches in

Part 1: The Bible

the Old and New Testaments.

The Bible is our answer, our friend, our companion, the written manifestation of what God has to say. It is God's gift to us!

CHAPTER 4

Proof that the Bible is the Word of God

Is there proof that the Bible is true? Doubters suppose the stories are not true. Skeptics claim the Bible is not accurate. Reluctant believers say it was written by humans. What evidence is there to prove the Bible is true?

The Bible actually *proves* itself to be true. The Bible proves what it claims about itself. The Word of God speaks from its own pages to reveal the answer as to whether it's all true. The Bible makes big and bold claims about its content. The Bible can and will answer for itself.

Then, after learning about the Source, the authors, the substance, the power, and everything that is in the Bible, everyone must decide whether they believe that the Bible is what it claims to be... the very Word of God, the mind of God, the revelation of God.

No more ignoring God's Word, no more lack of confidence in the Bible, no more avoidance or lack of interest in the Word of God, no more doubting.

If we question and doubt the veracity of the Bible, our faith will fail. On the other hand, if we are certain that the Bible is the Word of God, our faith will grow as we learn what

Part 1: The Bible

Scripture teaches.

Our faith is only as good as the object of our faith. If I have faith in my car, though my car is broken down, will my faith get me where I need to go? I can't "hope" my way to my destination. It all depends on the object of my faith, my car. If my faith is placed in a false god, a lifeless idol, a powerless statue (as in ancient pagan religions), is my faith going to help me? My faith is only as good as the person, place, or thing I'm trusting. Small faith in the one true God is better than great faith in a powerless idol or false belief system.

That is why it's so important to understand where the Bible came from, who wrote it, what's inside, and whether what is on the pages is trustworthy and true. If it is, then I have solid ground to stand on as I follow the Lord. I have a place to go for truth, learning, and growth. If I don't believe the Bible's testimony about itself, that it is the inspired Word of God, then my faith will shrink and die.

But how can we be sure?

Lack of knowledge is one of the biggest reasons people doubt the Bible. The Bible tells us in Hosea 4:6,

> *"...my people are destroyed from lack of knowledge."*

Without knowledge we will be stranded, confused, and left with only our perception of what is true. Fortunately, I was raised by a mother who loved the truth and taught me to love and seek the truth. One of the first things I learned as an adult Christian was this: *Faith is based on fact, not feelings.* Our faith is not just a crutch or a feel-good thing to hold onto in times of trouble. Oh no, it's much more than that. Our faith is based on the truth of God who revealed Himself to us through Scripture and the Lord Jesus Christ.

Since faith is based on what we know to be true, let's settle the "knowledge" part right here and now. Let's go through the facts that prove the Bible is exactly what it claims to be... the inspired Word of God.

HISTORICAL ACCURACY

The Bible contains the historical accounts of the Hebrew people, the events of their history, the kings of their nation, the prophets, the wars, and so much more. The Jewish scribes were meticulous in maintaining genealogies, recording history, and copying Scriptures. They had to follow many rules to make sure that not one detail was in error. Their facts had to be accurate as people's lives and futures depended on the information that was recorded. For example, individuals and families needed accurate records of their genealogies to prove who they were, what land they were entitled to, and from which tribe they originated. This was especially true of the Levitical priests serving in the temple. They were required to come from the tribe of Levi. The scribes were so meticulous that they never wrote from memory; they always copied directly from a scroll.

The scribes counted every letter and every word in order to check the manuscript. The editor would confirm that the middle word on each page of the copy matched the middle word on the manuscript being copied.[2]

Later, an editor would come and count every word and make sure nothing was missing or changed. There are so many other ways they ensured that copying manuscripts was exact and that no error was inadvertently made. The manuscripts were accurate and trustworthy.

As far as historical events, there have been details in the Bible that secular history couldn't verify until centuries later. For example, the book of Daniel mentions a Babylonian king named Belshazzar. For centuries, no one knew who Belshazzar was, as there didn't seem to be any record of him except in the Bible. Then in 1854, references to Belshazzar, son of Nabonidus, were discovered in Babylonian cuneiform inscriptions.[3]

Many facts, details, and dates are provided in the pages of the Bible that historians can compare with secular history records. Archaeological discoveries and historical records have confirmed thousands of details, dates, and names. If a detail has not been confirmed yet about a city or king or nation, it's best to just be patient. Secular history will catch up with the Bible at some point! The true and trustworthy historian is God Himself.

Secular history did catch up with the Bible in the 1940's and 1950's with the discovery of the Dead Sea Scrolls, which were found in the Qumran Caves near the Dead Sea. An astonishing number of scrolls and fragments of ancient Jewish Scriptures validated many books of the Old Testament as they are the oldest Biblical manuscripts ever found.

There is so much to be said about the historical veracity of the Bible that it would take much study and research to go through it. A better question to ask about whether the history is accurate is, what part of the Bible is *inaccurate*?

INTERNAL CONSISTENCY

Not only is the Bible accurate but it is *consistent*. I've heard people say, "The Bible has so many inconsistencies that

I don't believe it." Or they say, "There are things that are not true in the Bible." Or they may say, "The Bible contradicts itself."

My question to them is this, "I've read the Bible from start to finish and I've never found any inconsistencies. Can you tell me what you're referring to?" No one has ever been able to point out anything that would discredit the accuracy of the Bible.

Why is consistency so important? Because if the books of the Bible were written by human effort, there would be inconsistencies. Fallible people would make mistakes, add their opinions, editorialize, or lean toward their personal views while writing. But the Bible is surprisingly honest, transparent, factual, and certainly not written in a way that favors the writers or the people the authors wrote about. On the contrary, life stories are spared no messy details regarding adultery, lying, incest, murder, idolatry, and more.

The Bible is internally consistent throughout the books. Important doctrines and the message of reconciliation with God are solid, unchanging, and consistent throughout all of Scripture. When we consider that the records and writings were authored by over 40 different men over the course of over 1,500 years in three different continents, it would have been impossible for the authors to meet and plan the consistency held within their writings.

WITNESSES

Much of the Bible was written by eyewitnesses. We all know how important eyewitnesses can be. We will believe an event in question if we have a chance to hear from witnesses who were actually there. Deuteronomy 19:15b states,

PART 1: THE BIBLE

> *"A matter must be established by the testimony of two or three witnesses."*

Even today, eyewitness reports are very important in matters of historical and current events. How do we know history books contain the truth? Because of the records of eyewitnesses. How do we handle crimes in our justice system? By hearing accounts of incidents from eyewitnesses. After reading, listening, interviewing, and questioning the facts, people must choose what to believe based on the information provided. Witnesses are crucial to the process of making the right decisions about historical reports.

Many of the Old and New Testament writers were eyewitnesses to the events about which they wrote. Moses wrote the first five books of the Old Testament and personally experienced miracles and events that he recorded in Exodus. Other prophets were eyewitnesses of people's lives, events, wars, and more. The author of the book of Esther, most likely Esther's cousin Mordecai, witnessed and recorded the events described.

We know that Jesus was a true figure who walked on this earth. There were many eyewitnesses and records of Jesus, His life, ministry, death, and resurrection. Even secular history reports the person of Jesus of Nazareth who lived in the first century. Jesus is a real historical person, not a myth.

Two of the Gospel accounts in the New Testament were written by Matthew and John, both Disciples of Jesus who were eyewitnesses to His life and personally experienced the events they recorded. It is amazing for us to be able to read actual eyewitness accounts of the time Jesus was here on earth. Mark's account of the life of Jesus is included in the Gospels because he had firsthand interaction with and gained his information from the Apostles Peter and Paul. Luke was a doctor who traveled with the Apostle Paul on his missionary journeys. His account of Jesus is included in the Gospels because he interviewed eyewitnesses, including Jesus' mother, Mary.

Even though the Biblical events happened thousands of years ago, we rely on eyewitnesses to tell us what they saw and heard. As with all eyewitnesses, they explain things from their perspective; the details may vary slightly, which actually strengthens the case that their stories are not invented. The witnesses didn't corroborate to tell us exactly the same things. They didn't change their stories or leave things out or try to match their words with other witnesses. They were people who relayed what they saw and heard as they experienced the amazing events firsthand. Though their words were inspired by God, their writings flowed through their own personality and style.

FULFILLED PROPHECIES

It seems that people always want to look into the future and make predictions. We see it often in the news: predictions about the economy, the world, and the future. Such predictions are based on trends or expected future outcomes. Biblical prophecies are nothing like worldly predictions. A prophetic statement in the Bible is a word directly from the Lord and *will* come to pass. For some, this may be hard to believe. They may ask, "What about free will? What if someone makes a different decision that changes the outcome of what the Lord prophesied?"

God is powerful and sovereign over all of His creation. He knows everything including all thoughts and actions of people. His prophecies will come to pass. People have free will and make their decisions, but God knows everything before it comes to pass, which is why He can accurately state what will happen. He is also in full control, which means that at times, God steers the circumstances to accomplish His will. He can make things happen and stop things from happening. God can move circumstances and people according to His will. Man has free will, but God can intervene and overrule when He wants. No human can get in His way.

Fulfilled prophecy should leave us awestruck. After all, prophecies that have come to pass, exactly as a prophet of God has declared, are proof that there is a God and that the Biblical record is true. We can't ignore what that means. If prophecies were spoken about specific people and events to come, and hundreds of years later it happens exactly as the prophet said, that means that God is who He says and does what He says He will do. Our faith should never waver! *This is the Bible proving itself to be the Word of God.* After all, if prophecies don't come to pass, the credibility of the Bible falls apart on that problem alone. Nothing else could stand firm. Prophecies are one of the great pillars of the strong and powerful Word of God.

Many very specific prophecies spoken by the prophets of the Old Testament were fulfilled during ancient times. Many of these were predictions about wars, kings, and nations. Some took hundreds of years to be fulfilled; nevertheless, they came to pass exactly as predicted by God's prophets.

Here are a few of the many prophecies that have been fulfilled and are recorded in the Word of God.

The prophet Jeremiah predicted in 605 B.C. that the Jews would be taken into exile by the Babylonians for 70 years.

This prophecy came to pass in about 587 B.C., with the captivity ending after 70 years by a decree of King Cyrus allowing the Jews to return to Jerusalem. The prophet Isaiah also declared that Cyrus would release the Jews from captivity to go back to Jerusalem, and he prophesied this about 150 years before Cyrus was born! (Isaiah 44:28)

Isaiah also prophesied about the Messiah. These specific prophecies were fulfilled in Jesus. Isaiah chapter 9 tells us:

> *"And he will be called Wonderful Counselor, Mighty God, Everlasting Father, Prince of Peace." (vs. 6b)*

> *"He will reign on David's throne and over his kingdom, establishing and upholding it with justice and righteousness from that time on and forever." (vs. 7b)*

In Luke 1:32-33, the angel Gabriel appeared to Mary and spoke the same prophetic words to her. He told her that she would have a son that would be called the Son of God and that He will reign on the throne of David forever.

Isaiah 53:5 further prophesied about Jesus:
- ✢ "he was pierced for our transgressions"
- ✢ "he was crushed for our iniquities"
- ✢ "by his wounds we are healed"

It is amazing that these prophecies were spoken over 750 years before Christ was even born!

Jesus fulfilled over 300 prophecies. Some are very specific, such as how Jesus would be conceived (born of a virgin), where He would be born (Bethlehem), and that He would also live in Egypt.

Part 1: The Bible

> *"Therefore the Lord himself will give you a sign: The virgin will be with child and will give birth to a son, and will call him Immanuel." (Isaiah 7:14)*

Mary was a virgin pledged to be married when the angel Gabriel appeared to her saying she would have a son. She asked how it could be since she was a virgin. The angel answered,

> *"The Holy Spirit will come upon you and the power of the Most High will overshadow you. So the holy one to be born will be called the Son of God." (Luke 1:35)*

> *"But you, Bethlehem Ephrathah, though you are small among the clans of Judah, out of you will come for me one who will be ruler over Israel, whose origins are from old, from ancient times." (Micah 5:2)*

Although Nazareth was to be Jesus' hometown, He was born in Bethlehem due to a census that was being taken, forcing Mary and Joseph to travel there at the time of Jesus' birth. (Luke 2:7)

> *"When Israel was a child, I loved him, and out of Egypt I called my son." (Hosea 11:1)*

Mary and Joseph took Jesus to Egypt to escape King Herod's decree to kill baby boys. They lived there temporarily before moving back to Israel. (Matthew 2:14-15)

PROPHECY FULFILLMENT TODAY AND IN THE FUTURE

You may be interested to know that a very important event that was prophesied over 2,500 years ago came to pass in our modern day. The prophet Amos wrote,

> *"'I will plant Israel in their own land, never again to be uprooted from the land I have given them', says the Lord your God." (Amos 9:15)*

This prophecy was fulfilled in 1948 when the State of Israel was established. This is an amazing fulfillment of ancient prophecy that took place during my parents' lifetime!

We may witness more fulfillment of Biblical prophecy in our lifetime. The last book of the Bible, Revelation, contains many prophecies concerning the future. Some of these prophecies indicate circumstances that appear to be unfolding in our world today. The prophecies also explain what will take place at the end of the world. Many believe that the technology and other factors needed for some of these events to occur are materializing even today. Consider these statements of prophecy:

> "He also forced everyone, small and great, rich and poor, free and slave, to receive a mark on his right hand or on his forehead, so that no one could buy or sell unless he had the mark, which is the name of the beast or the number of his name."
> (Revelation 13:16-17)

What would it take to force everyone on earth to buy and sell using only a number? Would it mean using technology that exists today and is continuing to develop? Our world not only trades globally but relies less and less on cash. Numbers, chips, and scans are increasingly becoming the current method of transactions. How far off is our world from using a single number (or a mark) for each person? Revelation 14:9b-10 warns Believers not to take the mark of the beast.

The Word of God tells us that Jesus is coming again.

Recorded in the Bible are His prophecies and promises that He will return to earth.

> *"You also must be ready, because the Son of Man will come at an hour when you do not expect him." (Luke 12:40)*

> *"And if I go and prepare a place for you, I will come back and take you to be with me that you may also be where I am." (John 14:3)*

> *"'Men of Galilee,' they said, 'why do you stand here looking into the sky? This same Jesus, who has been taken from you into heaven, will come back in the same way you have seen him go into heaven.'" (Acts 1:11)*

The coming of the Lord Jesus was predicted hundreds of years before He was born. Now we hold on to the promise and the prophecies that Jesus is coming back!

SCIENCE

Another way the Bible proves itself to be the Word of God is by science. God is the creator of the heavens and the earth and the Author of the laws of nature that govern our universe. He gave mankind intellect and a desire to study and discover how His wondrous creation works. We should be in awe of God when complex and intriguing discoveries are made by scientists. God already knows it all, but scientists are always in the discovery process, striving to understand more about nature and the universe.

When did mankind discover the earth is actually round? A globe that hangs in space with no strings attached? The prophet Isaiah knew this fact over 750 years before Christ was born. Some may have speculated that the earth was round, but many wouldn't believe it until it was proven by science (and by explorers who actually traveled the globe). Yet the Bible revealed this fact in Isaiah 40:22a,

> *"He sits enthroned above the circle of the earth...."*

The book of Job was written hundreds of years before Christ and tells us in Job 26:7,

> *"He spreads out the northern skies over empty space; he suspends the earth over nothing."*

Today scientists understand the impact of the sun and the gravitational pull that keeps the earth stable in its orbit. Scientists caught up with the truth written in the book of Job.

God created the earth out of nothing. He spoke it into existence. Then, thousands of years later, we read in Hebrews 11:3 that what we see was made out of the unseen.

> *"By faith we understand that the universe was formed at God's command, so that what is seen was not made out of what was visible."*

Today scientists have powerful microscopes so they can study the atoms that are unseen to the naked eye.

How did the writers of ancient Scriptures know things about our world that scientists had not discovered yet? The only answer is that the Author of the Bible is the creator and sustainer of the entire universe.

JESUS BELIEVED THE SCRIPTURES

Another pillar of the truth of the Bible is that Jesus Himself believed in the credibility of the Scriptures. Here is what

Jesus said to the Pharisees who were persecuting Him:

> *"You diligently study the Scriptures because you think that by them you possess eternal life. These are the Scriptures that testify about me." (John 5:39)*

After the resurrection of Jesus, two of His followers were walking on the road to Emmaus. They were discussing all that had happened concerning the crucifixion and the account of the women who said the tomb was empty. Jesus appeared to them, though they were "kept from recognizing Him." He said to them,

> *"How foolish you are, and how slow of heart to believe all that the prophets have spoken! Did not the Christ have to suffer these things and then enter his glory?" (Luke 24:25-26)*

The next verse tells us,

> *"And beginning with Moses and all the Prophets, he explained to them what was said in all the Scriptures concerning himself." (vs. 27)*

Wow! Wouldn't you love to talk with Jesus and listen to Him explain the Scriptures to you?

Yes, Jesus believed the Scriptures. He spoke of events in the Old Testament as truth. Some people say that the incredible events of the Bible are simply fables or made-up legends. But Jesus believed the awesome miracles that are recorded in the Word of God. Jesus foretold His own death by using the prophet Jonah as an example.

> *"For as Jonah was three days and three nights in the belly of a huge fish, so the Son of Man will be three days and three nights in the heart of the earth."*
> *(Matthew 12:40)*

WOULD YOU LIKE MORE PROOF?

If historical accuracy, internal consistency, fulfilled prophecy, science, and the testimony of Jesus aren't enough to convince you that the Bible is the Word of God, there is one more way to prove that it is true. Ask your friend who is a Christian. Ask your pastor or another Believer that you know. Ask them about their experience with Jesus. Why do they believe? Ask them how their lives have changed. What happened to change their mind and turn them to the Lord?

When Christians explain how their lives have changed because of their faith in Jesus, you will hear modern day testimonies of the truth found in the Bible. That's why Christians are called "witnesses." Christians testify about what Jesus has done for them. We are witnesses to the truth of the Bible and the Gospel message of Jesus Christ. We tell our personal stories and those who hear our testimonies must decide whether they believe.

Believers have experienced what Jesus promised in the Word of God. We are forgiven and are now in a right relationship with God. We have been given the Holy Spirit to live inside of us, just as Jesus promised in Scripture. We know we've been changed, redeemed, and forgiven of our sin. The proof that the Bible is true is manifested in our own lives!

CHAPTER 5

The Inspired Scriptures

Who wrote the Bible, the bestselling book of all time? This book has compelled hateful enemies over the centuries to attempt to eliminate every single one. This book has caused people to be punished, persecuted, and even burned at the stake.

Who wrote this amazing, powerful, and compelling book that has caused so much havoc just by its mere existence?

Let's take a look at some of the writers of the books of the Bible. These are a few of the 40 different authors who wrote some of the 66 books that make up the Word of God.

Moses: Genesis, Exodus, Leviticus, Numbers, and Deuteronomy are attributed to Moses who was a Hebrew, raised in an Egyptian palace, worked later as a shepherd, then became a prophet and leader of God's people. These five books comprise the Torah, a portion of the Hebrew Bible, and are also referred to as the Pentateuch and the Law.

King David: Many of the psalms were written by King David. Some of David's psalms were written while he was fleeing for his life while being pursued by King Saul. When you read David's psalms, you'll understand why God called him a "man after my own heart."

King Solomon: Proverbs, Ecclesiastes, and Song of

Solomon were written by King David's son, Solomon. King Solomon is also known as the wisest man who ever lived.

Amos: The book of Amos was written by Amos who was a shepherd and farmer who became a prophet.

Samuel the prophet: 1 & 2 Samuel were presumably written by Samuel, who was a prophet and priest. The books of Samuel tell of the beginning of the monarchy of kings in the nation of Israel. One of the key characters in the books of Samuel is King David. It's important to learn about David's relationship with the Lord as Isaiah 9:7 prophesied that the coming Messiah will "reign on David's throne forever." David's kingdom will have no end!

Mordecai: The book of Esther is believed to have been written by her cousin, Mordecai. Esther was a humble, beautiful Jewish girl who became Queen of Persia. She bravely helped to save the entire Jewish nation from annihilation.

Luke: The book of Luke is attributed to Luke, the doctor who traveled with the Apostle Paul. Luke also wrote the book of Acts which documents the events after Jesus' resurrection and the beginning of the Christian church.

Matthew: A former tax collector who became a Disciple of Jesus and wrote one of the four Gospel accounts.

The Apostle Peter: 1 & 2 Peter are attributed to having been written by Peter, the outspoken fisherman who was a Disciple of Jesus and became the leader of the early Christian church.

The Apostle Paul: The Epistles in the New Testament were written by the Apostle Paul, who wrote 13 of the 27 books in the New Testament. Originally these books were written as letters to the early Christian churches and some to specific individuals. Paul was persecuted and thrown into prison, where he wrote four of his letters: Ephesians, Philippians, Colossians, and Philemon. The rest of the books that Paul wrote are Romans, 1 & 2 Corinthians, Galatians, 1 & 2 Thessalonians, 1 & 2 Timothy, and Titus. Paul wrote and clarified Christian doctrine amidst many false teachings that were going around at that time.

Jude and James: Each wrote books titled in their names. It is believed that both Jude and James were half-brothers of Jesus. (Matthew 6:3)

The Apostle John: The book of Revelation was written by the Apostle John while on the island of Patmos. Revelation includes letters to Christian churches that were dictated by Jesus Himself. John also wrote the Gospel of John and 1, 2, & 3 John.

You may be thinking, "These are mere men! Fishermen, shepherds, a tax collector, a doctor, and a farmer? They are people just like you and me!"

You are right. They were mere men, human beings just like you and me. They were Believers who had faith and were willing to be used by God to further His Kingdom. How is it possible that mere men could have written letters or history or songs or eyewitness accounts that eventually became part of the bestselling book of all time?

Was it simply a group of various men who thought they had some good ideas to write? Was it the prophets who wanted others to read their predictions of the future? Was it fishermen or a doctor or a tax collector whose lives were changed by a humble Jewish miracle worker who walked the earth over 2,000 years ago? Was it an outspoken Pharisee who persecuted Believers, but then fell off his horse on the Damascus Road, blinded by the light of Jesus and then miraculously converted to Christianity?

The writers of this powerful collection of books were not simply men who wanted to record their experiences with God. Oh, they physically wrote with their hands in their vocabulary and style and personality. But the actual writer of the bestselling book of all time is *God Himself*. The God of the universe and Creator of all things. Out of His great love for mankind (the masterpiece of His creation), He *supernaturally* worked through mere men to put His message into words.

Sounds simple, right? The all-powerful God worked through human beings to get His message into a format that we could actually read! Well, it wasn't quite that easy. The book that you hold in your hands wasn't just written, printed, published, and distributed all around the world as other books might have been. The entire process was attacked by so many enemies that it required miracles for the Bible to be available to us today.

The same God who miraculously breathed His words onto the pages of Scripture is the same God who miraculously preserved His Word through centuries of persecution. Nothing and no one can destroy God's Word. His Word is eternal.

> *"The grass withers and the flowers fall, but the word of our God endures forever." (Isaiah 40:8)*

How did God accomplish the written record, putting His infinite mind into finite words and the unfolding of His revelation through frail human beings?

GOD-BREATHED

2 Timothy 3:16-17 says,

> *"All Scripture is God-breathed and is useful for teaching, rebuking, correcting and training in righteousness, so that the man of God may be thoroughly equipped for every good work."*

God-breathed. God-inspired. All Scripture, although written by men, was divinely inspired. The word "inspired" in the original language was much stronger than our English word. We say that we feel inspired to write or create something. But our word for "inspiration" is not the same meaning as what the original Biblical text means. God-inspired, or God-breathed, means that the breath of God was blown or breathed out so that the very words of God were written.

We can't take that lightly. The Holy Spirit didn't simply inspire the writers and then, after being inspired, the writers took off and wrote their own words. No! The Holy Spirit was fully involved, divinely influencing, guiding, and controlling in order to produce the writings, the record of the mind of God, the truth of God, and His revelation to mankind. This is one of the pillars of the foundation of Christianity. If you don't believe that the Scriptures are "God-breathed" and inspired by the Holy Spirit, then you do not believe the claims of Christianity.

The Greek word for God-breathed is "theopneustos." "Theo" means God and "pneustos" comes from "pneuma" which pertains to breath or spirit. The most correct meaning is "breathe out" as opposed to "breathe in." God breathed the words out and His very words were put in written form.

How did God accomplish this? At times, God spoke directly to an individual and told him what to write, as in Revelation 14:13. Other times, the writers were moved and controlled by the Spirit. They were "carried along" by the Holy

Spirit.

2 Peter 1:20-21 explains,

> *"Above all, you must understand that no prophecy of Scripture came about by the prophet's own interpretation. For prophecy never had its origin in the will of man, but men spoke from God as they were carried along by the Holy Spirit."*

THE MEN THAT GOD INSPIRED

How can a human being write by the inspiration of the Holy Spirit? Is it possible for the Holy Spirit to guide and control the writers of Scripture, yet allow them to use their own styles of writing? Absolutely. The phrase "carried along by the Holy Spirit" means that the writers were *moved and controlled* by the Spirit. In this way, the writers expressed words using their own language, style, and perspective (such as the Gospels), yet God was sovereignly in control of the writing.

Thus, the writers of God's mind and revelation on the pages of Scripture were inspired and controlled in a very powerful way by the Holy Spirit. God's Word was written and the result was exactly what God planned, using human instruments. God could have written it without the human hand and pen, but He loves working with and through people. This is how He works and how He operates in His creation. And with the written Word, God moved, through the power of the Holy Spirit, to place His words in their minds, help them recall events, and inspire them to accurately word their writings. The Holy Spirit burned in their hearts with divine inspiration and accuracy to get the complete revelation of God into written form.

THE BIBLE IS THE WORD OF GOD

We may hear people say, "The Bible contains the Word of God." The Bible does not "contain" the Word of God. The Bible *is* the Word of God.

This is the foundation of the Christian faith. Jesus stated in Matthew 5:18:

> *"I tell you the truth, until heaven and earth disappear, not the smallest letter, not the least stroke of a pen, will by any means disappear from the Law until everything is accomplished."*

In those words, Jesus emphasized that every word is from God and will be accomplished as written.

Since every word is so important, God commands us not to add or take away from what is written.

> *"Do not add to what I command you and do not subtract from it but keep the commands of the Lord your God that I give you." (Deuteronomy 4:2)*

Revelation 22:18-19 tells us how serious it is for anyone who does change the Word of God:

> *"I warn everyone who hears the words of the prophecy of this book: if anyone adds anything to them, God will add to him the plagues described in this book. And if anyone takes words away from this book of prophecy, God will take away from him his share in the tree of life and in the holy city, which are described in this book."*

Below are additional verses admonishing those who add words or take words away from the Bible:

PART 1: THE BIBLE

> *"Do not add to his words, lest he rebuke you and prove you a liar." (Proverbs 30:6)*

> *"See that you do all I command you; do not add to it or take away from it." (Deuteronomy 12:32)*

The Bible warns against treating the Word of God as if written by men, therefore able to be changed by men. God has not left us with such a weak, frail, and flimsy pillar on which to rest our faith. God was in control of His own words and His own message to the masterpiece of His creation.

GOD SPEAKS TO MANKIND

God still speaks to mankind through His Word. His words are alive, filled with power, and will pierce the hearts of those who seek Him. Through the words on the pages of the Bible, we hear God's voice speaking to our particular circumstances and helping us through the challenges of life. Each day we can hear God's voice through the very words of His message to us.

God's heart is to communicate with us and to be in an intimate relationship with us. God speaks to us through His Word, so if we want to know what God's mind is on the matters that concern us, we must read the Bible.

WHY DOESN'T GOD JUST TALK OUT LOUD?

In ancient times, before the written Word was available to people, God did speak out loud. At times, prophets received messages from God by an audible voice. That was one way He spoke to His people in those days. God also sent angels to impart a verbal message or instruction to His servants. Or God would send a message in a dream to certain people. Even today, God may speak to us through another individual or impress on our hearts a message or instruction regarding His will. But the primary way that God speaks today is on the pages of Scripture. In fact, if we ever hear a message that contradicts Scripture, we will know the message is not of God.

The Bible is our link to God and learning who He really is. It is His way of communicating His mind, His heart, and His revelation to us. As we respond to this mighty and powerful book, we walk by faith, trusting what it says and trusting the Author of the Bible.

CHAPTER 6

The Law, Laws, and More Laws

If you have ever read the entire Bible from start to finish, you may have been a little bored when reading through the specific laws and commands of God in the first five books of the Old Testament. I suppose that some might think that God was being unreasonable, strict, or harsh. Why so many laws? Why such detail?

The answer is very simple and is found in Deuteronomy 4:1 which says,

> *"Hear now, O Israel, the decrees and laws I am about to teach you. Follow them so that you may live and may go in and take possession of the land that the Lord, the God of your fathers, is giving you."*

+ God gave the Law because of His great love for His people.
+ God gave the Law to demonstrate who He is.
+ God gave the Law to teach His standards of behavior.
+ God gave the Law because He is a just God.

But how do these specific and, at times, rigid laws show God's love? Consider parents who implement rules as they raise their children. Do they have rules because they love their children or hate them? Of course, they love them and want them to be healthy, safe, wise, productive, and joyful.

The context of this time in the lives of the Hebrew people was that they had just been freed from 400 years of slavery under the Egyptians. That's a long time! That's about 20 generations of people who worked as slaves from sun up to sun down, seven days a week, year after year after year. Finally, the Hebrew people were freed by God Himself, through Moses and a series of mighty miracles that you can read about in the book of Exodus.

Now life was about to change from hard toil with no pleasure, no cultural traditions, and no temple worship to a new life full of freedom, hope, and joy. No longer would they be ruled by slave masters who abused them, but by one ruler, their God who loved them. Everything was about to change. But what changes would the people make? All they knew was slavery, abuse, and hopelessness.

God was going to teach them how to live in freedom and how to steward all of the blessings He planned to provide to them. God would explain to the Hebrew people how they should live and how to be successful in this new system of freedom, morality, and structure. He did this through the Law, disseminating His instructions through His servant, Moses. The myriad of detailed laws covered everything including worship, justice, mercy, health, property, inheritance, morality, and the legal system. The people had no experience with many of these aspects of life. They didn't know how to buy, sell, or manage property because they had never owned land. They didn't know how food related to health because they only ate what was available. Now God would explain through the Law how to manage these aspects of life in order to flourish and be blessed. It makes sense that God would start from scratch and disseminate a set of rules and boundaries for a whole new way of life.

THE LAW INTERPRETED BY JESUS

Over the years, there were many traditions and understandings of the Law that were added to the original Law that God gave to Moses. Those interpretations became known as the Oral Law, which was based on tradition and was not given by God. The Oral Law was written by men and referred to ways in which the commandments were to be obeyed or lived out in daily life.

The Pharisees (religious leaders) relied heavily on the Oral Law which soon became cumbersome, unreasonable, and even impossible to obey. Jesus' interpretation of the Law contrasted sharply with the interpretations of the religious leaders of the day. We read about Jesus' disagreements with the Pharisees in the Gospels. There are many instances of Jesus confronting them concerning matters of the Law. Jesus strongly rebuked the Pharisees to correct their traditions and legalistic interpretations of God's Law.

The confrontations caused the Pharisees to hate Jesus. They were angry when Jesus healed on the Sabbath, which was against the Oral Law but not against God's Law. Jesus corrected the Pharisees when they criticized Him for being merciful and healing the sick on the Sabbath. Jesus' interpretation was that mercy should prevail. He told the Pharisees,

> *"The Sabbath was made for man, not man for the Sabbath." (Mark 2:27)*

Jesus helps us to understand God's Law by His answer to

a Pharisee's question about which commandment is the greatest. Jesus answered by stating,

> *"Love the Lord your God with all your heart and with all your soul and with all your mind. This is the first and greatest commandment. And the second is like it: 'Love your neighbor as yourself.' All the Law and the Prophets hang on these two commandments." (Matthew 22:37-40)*

Jesus explained that if people obey those two commandments, they will be fulfilling God's expectations explained in the entire Law.

Jesus taught the proper way to understand God's Law. He stated in Matthew 5:17 that He didn't come to erase or nullify the Law, rather to fulfill it.

THE LAW AND SALVATION

Some believe that people in the Old Testament were saved by the Law, and we are now saved by grace. The truth is, salvation has always been by grace. The Old Testament patriarch, Abraham, is an example of righteousness that is by faith, not by works.

> *"Abram believed the Lord, and he credited it to him as righteousness." (Genesis 15:6)*

It was Abram's (Abraham's) faith that God credited to him as righteousness. God knew that no human being could keep the entire Law. Everyone has fallen short of its requirements.

The Law in the Old Testament was not given so that people would work, work, work to earn salvation. On the contrary, the Law was given so that they would know what sin is and understand that they were sinners. The Law would teach them God's standards of righteousness and help them recognize their need for a Savior.

The Apostle Paul explains in Romans 3:20, "Therefore no one will be declared righteous in his sight by observing the law; rather, through the law we become conscious of sin." The Law demonstrates the holiness of God. Furthermore, Paul tells us in Galatians 3:24,

> "So the law was put in charge to lead us to Christ that we might be justified by faith."

Instead of the phrase "put in charge," some versions say the Law was our "schoolmaster" or "guardian."

And so we study the Law, but we are saved by grace. And even in the Old Testament, those who believed and entered into a relationship with God were saved by the grace of God.

THE LAW WRITTEN ON OUR HEARTS

Where is the Law in the life of the Believer? The Bible tells us that the Law is now written on our hearts. Hebrews 8:10 tells us that God will "put my laws in their minds and write them on their hearts." The indwelling Holy Spirit guides Believers to obedience to the will of God.

God's expectations of holiness will never change. The Law, the heart of God, the message of God to us, will endure. The Law is not our enemy; it is the instrument that God uses to explain and proclaim how much we need our Savior!

CHAPTER 7

Translations of the Bible

The last command of Jesus before He left the earth was,

> "Go into all the world and preach the good news to all creation." (Mark 16:15)

Since the original writings of the Scriptures were in the Hebrew, Aramaic, and Greek languages, translations were necessary. God intended that His Word be spread throughout the world, thus the inspired Holy Word of God would eventually be translated into thousands of different languages.

TRANSLATIONS NEEDED!

The Septuagint, a Greek translation of the Hebrew Bible, was widely used for the Old Testament. The translation process was completed around the second century B.C. The first major translation of the New Testament was from Greek to Syriac, which was the language of Damascus. This translation took place around 170 A.D. About the year 382 A.D., the Pope commissioned his secretary, Jerome, to create a translation in Latin. Jerome completed the Latin Vulgate, which was the standard used by the Catholic Church for the next 1,000 years.[4]

Translating the Bible from its original text into other

languages sounds straightforward and relatively easy, right? Not so, as there were two major challenges that have existed throughout the centuries regarding Bible translation. The first challenge was the persecution and the attempts to thwart and block early translations of the Bible, particularly the translation into English. At that time, church leaders did not think that ordinary people should have access to the Scriptures. The second challenge was and continues to be the word-for-word translation from the original text to another language.

PERSECUTION OF TRANSLATORS

As the need arose for the original text of the Scriptures to be translated into Anglo-Saxon English and eventually modern English, so did the problems and persecutions.

In the middle of the 14th century, John Wycliffe translated the Bible into the common language. After he died, his following grew, and so did the persecution. The main reason for the persecution was that it was illegal in England, under the Catholic Church at that time, to translate the Bible. It was thought that the translators were heretical and would change the Scriptures.

The goal of the translators was to provide the Bible to the common people in their language. There is much to be studied regarding the topic of the intense persecution as there are various records and viewpoints. What we know for sure is that the translators were severely persecuted and even martyred for their efforts to translate the Bible.

William Tyndale worked on translating the New Testament into English in the 1500's. Tyndale was committed to making the Bible available to the everyday person. He completed translating books of the Old Testament before He was

TRANSLATIONS OF THE BIBLE

martyred for his efforts and accomplishments of the translations. Tyndale was accused of heresy by certain leaders of the Catholic Church, mainly because they wanted to maintain the Church as the only authority. He was killed and his body was burned at the stake. It is reported that his final words, which he cried out in a loud voice, were, "Lord, open the King of England's eyes." His prayer was answered several years later when the King of England allowed the Bible to be printed in England.[5]

After Tyndale was executed, other people continued his mission of getting the Bible printed and made available. John Rogers, who was a friend of Tyndale, produced the Matthews Bible also in the 1500's. Queen Mary had Rogers burned at the stake for being a Protestant. She was referred to as "Bloody Mary" for her blood-stained efforts to change England back to Catholicism.

Because of the persecution, many Protestants fled to Geneva and other areas. Then, for the first time, a team of translators created the Geneva Bible and numbered the verses, as well as added commentaries and maps.[6]

Chapters had already been added to the Bible several hundred years before the Geneva Bible. Stephen Langon, Archbishop of Canterbury, is credited with dividing the Bible into chapters in order to find passages more easily.

In 1611, King James VI of Scotland desired a version of the Bible for all Christians. He used a large group of translators to accomplish this task. It is believed that this event was the answer to William Tyndale's prayer. Many Christians still use the King James version or a more modern version called the New King James version.

The printing press was invented during the 15th century,

which made the Bible much more available to people. The Gutenberg Bible was the first book printed on Gutenberg's press!

TRANSLATING THE LANGUAGE

Those of us who have spent time learning another language understand that not only are the words unique and different, but there are changes in the composition of the sentences. Some languages place the adjective before the noun, some after the noun, some have different verb placement, and some use more complex sentence structures. There are many nuances with various languages that make translating from one language to another very challenging.

So it is with Bible translations. The original manuscripts were written in Hebrew, Aramaic, and Greek. The composition of sentences in the Greek language is more complex than our English language. And all three of the original languages were written with a different alphabet!

The topic of languages and translations is very broad and there is much information available to study how translations are accomplished. For the purpose of *Best Seller*, a brief overview will give you a glimpse and help you to appreciate the efforts of so many people to translate the Bible into over 2,500, and possibly closer to 3,000 different languages.

BIBLE TRANSLATIONS AND VERSIONS

There have been amazing efforts to translate the Bible word for word, without losing the original intent or meaning. Where words could not be precisely translated, the translators have strived to find the most accurate words that would not allow for any loss of meaning or diminishment of the intent of the original writer.

The same challenge exists for translators each time a new version is created. They make every effort to be accurate in the translation as well as finding the right words that will give the reader the ability to understand the text.

Some versions are better than others, and most Christians who have a choice of available translations have their preferred or favorite version. However, we must be discerning regarding any translation that has actually changed the words that distort the meaning of the original text.

The New International Version (NIV) has been an easy-to-understand version that I have relied on for years. With ease of access to other versions on the internet, I've enjoyed reading other versions for comparison and enhanced understanding of passages. I know many Christians who have other favorite versions, such as the New American Standard Bible (NASB) or the English Standard Version (ESV). Some Christians believe the New King James Version (NKJV) is a good literal translation. Thankfully, most of the translations available have been created with the goal of maintaining the meaning of the original Hebrew, Greek, and Aramaic languages.

Scripture is the foundation of our knowledge and realm of learning. We should also attend a Bible-based church and fellowship with other Christians. We can learn a lot by studying and delving into Scripture with a group of Believers.

PARAPHRASED VERSIONS OF THE BIBLE

A translation is an effort to change the original words into a different language while maintaining accuracy, but a paraphrase is not a word-for-word translation from one language to another. A paraphrase seeks to capture the substance of the text and is written with an emphasis on the meaning rather than the specific words.

A paraphrase is a support tool to help with understanding the text but Christians should always have a word-for-word translation that they rely on as their primary source for their studies of the Bible. A paraphrase is not intended to be the only source of Scripture for those who are studying the Bible.

STUDY BIBLE, CONCORDANCE, AND COMMENTARY

It is very good to have a hard copy of the Bible so that you can underline and make notations while you read. A study Bible is highly recommended because it contains helpful notes on the bottom of the pages as you read through Scripture. These notes help the reader understand the context of the passages as well as offer interesting details that take the reader deeper into the text. Some Bibles include maps or other helpful information, including cross references, as tools to help the reader.

A concordance is a study tool that lists words and references where the words can be found in Scripture. This is helpful when you know the topic or the word you are looking for, but don't know where to find it.

A commentary provides an interpretation and analysis of passages in the Bible. You will find a commentary very helpful to use alongside your Bible as you study. Commentaries provide insights into a passage, the author, who the author was writing to, and the history and the culture of the time. These insights help us with passages that we might not understand without the additional help from theologians who have studied the related information surrounding the text.

THE INERRANT WORD OF GOD

As we seek discernment while studying the Bible, I believe that our Christian history, the core beliefs of mainline Christianity, and a good literal translation of the Bible will help us to learn the truth. When we hear of "new" ideas or variations of our historical Christian beliefs, that should be the first sign of a possible heresy. The truth we cling to is the Bible. We desire to study the original wording of the Bible and the original intent of the writers. The Bible is inerrant in its original text. Many Christian churches affirm this fact in their statements of belief. They profess that the Word of God is without error in the original writings. This is a core doctrine of Christianity; therefore, Christians must reject "new" variations that distort the Word of God.

Never take for granted that Bibles are plentiful and available in thousands of languages around the world. I treasure my Bible because I am so grateful for the sacrifices of those who translated the Scriptures into English. They were willing to get it done, even in the face of persecution and death. The Bible on our bookshelves in our own language was made available through tears, suffering, and blood. We should be very humbled and grateful.

CHAPTER 8

Price of the Bestselling Book

Although many of us love the Word of God, there are people who hate the Bible. We don't really see that kind of hatred toward books of other religions. But there is something about the Bible that makes people want to do more than just despise it, they want to destroy it. They want the Word of God out of their sight, as far away as possible.

This persecution serves to support that the Bible is the truth. After all, if it were a fairy tale with made up stories or simply a compilation of man-made writings with no purpose or power, why would it be so important for people to abolish it?

Many people hate the Bible because the words on the pages convict us of sin. The Bible teaches us how to live, shows us the behaviors that God calls sin, warns us of rejecting God, and calls us to believe and submit to a Holy God. It's like turning a light on in a dark world of sin. Who wants the light that pierces the darkness of sin and reveals the truth? Many people prefer to continue their sinful deeds in the dark.

In the United States, we don't feel the persecution as much as people do in some other countries. We can walk into a bookstore and find this bestselling book and purchase it. We are free to study it, talk about it, and carry it around in public.

PART 1: THE BIBLE

Because the Bible is so readily available and people have the ability to own a copy or find the Bible online, they perhaps take it for granted. Some people have the Bible stuck in a bookcase in their home and haven't opened it for years. This bestseller might even be sitting on the coffee table, unnoticed, and collecting dust.

If we only knew what it cost to have this precious, valuable book available to hold in our hands! The price was high. In fact, many of the authors of the Bible paid the highest price. Their tears, their blood, their lives. Some were persecuted, imprisoned, tortured and killed. Understanding the immeasurable value of the Scriptures, they paid the highest possible price to write, preserve, and circulate the precious Word of God.

There are those who say, "Someday I'll read it." Or they comment, "I tried to read it once and it was just too hard to understand." God's Word? *Maybe, but I'm pretty busy right now.* God's message to mankind? *I've got better things to do.* The truth that guides our lives? *My life is pretty good, let's talk about this later.* The Gospel of Salvation? *Possibly, but I'll think about it when I'm ready.*

We should never forget the history of the sacrifice, the effort, and the cost that was made so that you and I could even have the option of deciding whether we think this book is important enough to read. It is life-giving medicine for our souls! Wouldn't it be terrible if you needed special medicine to heal your dying body and it simply wasn't available? Oh, it exists but you can't have any of it! That wouldn't be acceptable to you. And not having access to the Holy, powerful, life-giving truth of the God who created you shouldn't be acceptable to us either.

That's exactly what the writers of the Bible and the Church's forefathers thought and what motivated them to do whatever it took to get the saving message of the Gospel out to a hurting world. They endured persecution and martyrdom for the sake of the Word of God.

THE PERSECUTION PERSISTS TODAY

Millions of Christians around the world are suffering persecution even today for their beliefs. It's hard to believe, isn't it? Yet over the centuries, Christians have been persecuted, jailed, and killed for their faith in the Lord Jesus. There are countries today that ban or restrict people from owning a Bible. In fact, in some countries where the Bible is banned, people are jailed or put to death for having a Bible in their possession.

Yet faithful Christians around the world would rather be imprisoned or die than renounce their faith and or give up their copy of the precious Word of God.

THE PRICE OF THE BESTSELLING BOOK OF ALL TIME

Periodically we are reminded of the sacrifices made by those who fought in wars to defend our nation and our freedoms. We celebrate holidays throughout the year that remind us of the price that was paid for our freedom, just in case we begin to take it for granted. What is the price of freedom? Well, there are very high prices. Thousands of people had to leave their families at home, go far away to fight, endure indescribable hardships, and ultimately shed their own blood in order for you and me to be spared from being overtaken by evil oppressors. The price of freedom is pain, suffering, sacrifice, and bloodshed.

What is the price of the Word of God? History reveals that

the price to get the Old and New Testaments written included pain, suffering, sacrifice, and bloodshed. But let's focus on the bloodshed, as that has permeated the Bible's story from the very beginning. We have the writings of the prophets in the Old Testament. Many of them suffered greatly as they preached and prophesied. Some were tortured and martyred. Jesus' Disciples also paid the highest price for their contribution to Christianity and the Word of God, with many persevering in spreading the Gospel message until they were martyred. The Apostle Paul, the writer of many of the New Testament books, was martyred for his faith.

PRICELESS

My Bible is not just one book of many in my collection of books. I've owned the same Bible for decades and have studied its contents for years. The margins are filled with my handwritten notes, insights, prayers, and answers to prayers. I have read and continue to read from Genesis to Revelation. I seek its wisdom by reading it daily. God has spoken to me clearly through the pages of His Word. The Bible has helped me, taught me, comforted me, blessed me, and brought me into an intimate relationship with God. Millions of Christians over the centuries have also experienced these life-changing blessings from the Word of God.

What is the price of the love and knowledge and peace and life that the Bible gives us? Would all the silver and gold in the world be able to provide that? No, this book was bought with the precious blood of the persevering saints who were led and equipped by the Holy Spirit to get the Bible into my hands so I could know God and have life.

That means that the Bible is *priceless*.

PART 2

The Themes of the Bible

CHAPTER 9

Themes within the Bible

If you wanted proof that the Bible is the Word of God, what information would you need? What would it take for you to be certain that all the books were inspired by God and that the Bible is truly the revelation of God written on the pages of Scripture?

One of the ways that the Bible proves itself to be inspired by God is that there are themes that flow throughout the pages. Remember, the books of the Bible were actually written over the course of 1,500 years. Many of its authors didn't even know each other, let alone live in the same century.

How is it possible for themes to flow through the Bible if there was no collaboration, planning, meetings, or consultations? Yet the character of God and important themes flow powerfully through the pages of Scripture. The only way that strong themes throughout the books of the Bible could possibly be consistent and accurate would be by Divine inspiration.

The themes of the Bible provide evidence and proof that the Word of God is faithful and true.

I've heard it said, "Let the Bible speak for itself. The Word of God explains itself." I love the fact that we don't have to rely on a person or a scholar or a theological expert to prove to us that the Bible is genuinely the Word of God. The Bible proves itself to be true and genuine. We let the Bible talk to us, tell us the truth, prove its validity, and teach us about its trustworthiness.

WHY THEMES ARE SO IMPORTANT

Themes of the Bible are important for several reasons. The themes that we recognize as we study Scripture *prove the consistency of God's character.* As we read each of the books of the Bible, we learn about God's character, how He responds to people, how He acts in situations, and how He can be depended upon. Through the many writings, the themes prove to us that God is real and we come to know His personality, character, and what is important to Him.

Another reason that the themes of the Bible are so important is because they *emphasize and teach us what God wants us to know.* For example, the theme of reconciliation with God flows throughout the Bible. From Genesis to Revelation, we read about God's desire to reconcile people to Himself. We learn about our sinfulness and separation from a Holy God and His provision for forgiveness and reconciliation. The theme of reconciliation with God is written about, explained, and even pictured through symbolism on the pages of Scripture. When we learn about reconciliation in the various ways it is presented, we learn all that God wants us to know about it.

Lastly, the themes give us a *depth of understanding* that one sentence or one explanation can't fully express. In other words, the theme is so profound that learning one simple explanation won't take us to the depth of what we need to learn. Weaving the theme throughout Scripture helps us to go continuously deeper into the mind of God concerning the truth

He wants us to understand. For example, we can read that Jesus is our Redeemer. Or, we can read throughout the pages of Scripture the examples of how God has redeemed people, situations, and circumstances. We read about the true story of Ruth in the Old Testament, a woman in a foreign land with no hope but whose life was changed by a Kinsman Redeemer. The story of her life takes us deep into the truth of what a Redeemer does for those He loves. After we read Ruth's story, our hearts are filled with a better understanding of what Jesus did for us on the cross. And we certainly have deeper insight when we read passages such as Exodus 15:13a which says,

> *"In your unfailing love you will lead the people you have redeemed."*

The themes of the Bible provide one unified message about who God is and what His plan is for mankind. Themes are evidence that prove there is one Author of the Scriptures.

CHAPTER 10

The Theme of the Covenants

"Covenant" sounds like an ancient term, doesn't it? We usually don't refer to our modern day legal agreements as covenants. But essentially that is what a covenant is, a legal agreement, a form of a contract, a binding promise. A contract is impersonal, whereas a covenant is much more personal and focuses more on the relationship. What is so special about a covenant in the Bible is that one of the parties involved in the agreement is God!

Some covenants are conditional and usually the condition is: "If you obey." Other covenants are unconditional, such as the Abrahamic Covenant. God's promise to Abraham for descendants and land was unconditional. God promised Abraham that his descendants would be as numerous as the stars and that land would be given to them. The "Promised Land" that God swore to Abraham is the land of Israel.

THE OLD AND NEW COVENANTS

You may be familiar with the Old Covenant and the New Covenant. Some think of the Old and New Testaments as the Old and New Covenants. That is because the word "testament" comes from a Greek word that carries the meaning of covenant. But actually, the Old Testament contains the Old Covenant and the New Testament contains New Covenant.

The Old Covenant refers to the Law which includes the Ten Commandments plus the other laws that were given through Moses (1400 B.C.). These are recorded in the Old Testament. "Thou shalt not..." showed how to behave, what to do, and what not to do. The Old Covenant is also referred to as the Mosaic Covenant and was a covenant between God and the Israelite people. The Mosaic Covenant included the sacrificial system of offering animals to atone for sin. It was a conditional covenant that required God's people to obey the Law that was given to Moses. If they obeyed and followed the laws, they would be blessed.

The Old Covenant (the Law) explained what was important to God, what was right and wrong, and the standard of morality by which the people were expected to live. When the people sinned, the sacrificial system required the shedding of the blood of an innocent animal as atonement. According to the Law in Leviticus 17:11, the shedding of blood was necessary for forgiveness.

The Old Covenant prepared the way for Jesus because it taught people the meaning of innocent blood being shed to atone for their sins. It guided God's people to understand the holiness of God, the sinfulness of mankind, and the need for forgiveness in order to be in fellowship with God.

The Old Covenant laid the foundation for the New Covenant of Grace, which is the promise of God to forgive our sins by grace alone through faith in Jesus Christ. Jesus atoned for our sins by shedding His blood on the cross. Hebrews 9:22b says,

> *"...without the shedding of blood there is no forgiveness."*

Jesus, the Lamb of God, shed His blood for the complete, permanent, and final atonement for our sin.

The New Covenant is not based on works; its basis is the grace of God through faith in Jesus. Ephesians 2:8-9 explains,

> *"For it is by grace you have been saved, through faith—and this not from yourselves, it is the gift of God—not by works, so that no one can boast."*

Those who believe that good works and obedience will earn them the right to eternal life have a wrong understanding of what the Bible teaches. Works are important, and we shouldn't stop doing good works! But good works are the *fruit* of salvation, they are not the price we pay to *earn* salvation.

Here is an easy-to-understand comparison of the Old Covenant (Law) and the New Covenant (Grace):

- ✛ The Old Covenant revealed sin.
- ✛ The New Covenant covers our sin with grace.
- ✛ The Old Covenant brought condemnation for sin.
- ✛ The New Covenant brings righteousness by faith.
- ✛ The Old Covenant was impossible to completely obey.
- ✛ The New Covenant requires that we place our faith in Jesus.
- ✛ The Old Covenant was temporary.
- ✛ The New Covenant is everlasting.
- ✛ The purpose of the Old Covenant was to point to Christ.
- ✛ The New Covenant is fulfilled in Christ.
- ✛ The Old Covenant was between God and the

Israelites.
+ The New Covenant is offered to everyone.
+ The Law was written on tablets in the Old Covenant.
+ The New Covenant includes God's promise to write His Law in our hearts.
+ The Old Covenant commanded obedience to the law.
+ The New Covenant enables us to obey by choice through the power of the Holy Spirit.

IS THE OLD COVENANT WORTHLESS NOW?

Some believe Christ invalidated the Law by granting forgiveness through repentance and faith in Him. Why would we care any longer about the antiquated system of Law?

The Apostle Paul answers this common question. He said in Romans 7:7 that we wouldn't know what sin is without the Law. "What shall we say, then? Is the law sinful? Certainly not! Indeed, I would not have known what sin was except through the law. For I would not have known what coveting really was if the law had not said, 'Do not covet.'"

Jesus made it clear that the Law would never be abolished until every detail has been fulfilled. Jesus said in Matthew 5:17-18,

> *"Do not think that I have come to abolish the Law or the Prophets; I have not come to abolish them but to fulfill them. I tell you the truth, until heaven and earth disappear, not the smallest letter, not the least stroke of a pen, will by any means disappear from the Law until everything is accomplished."*

Just because the Law was given in the Mosaic Covenant centuries ago to an ancient group of people doesn't mean it is not relevant to the entire world. The Ten Commandments continue to be God's standard of morality even in our society today. The system of justice in our country is heavily based on this ancient set of laws given to Moses on Mount Sinai. Even though we are under the New Covenant of Grace, God's standards of righteousness are evident in the framework of morality defined by the Old Covenant.

Perfect and sinless, Jesus fulfilled the requirements of the Law. Now there is only one requirement under the New Covenant. Faith in Jesus!

THE SERIOUSNESS OF COVENANTS

Not only are the covenants of God filled with blessings for His people, but there are serious consequences for the parties involved if they are not obedient to their part of the agreement. I daresay that the punishment for breaking a conditional covenant with God is actually worse than if the person committed the same sin with no covenant. Why? Because when God moves in close and invites His people into a covenant with Him, it becomes a very special relationship. It is a powerful promise from God that He will do something extraordinary.

Whether conditional or unconditional, a covenant is explained and ratified by a sign. Among the signs given to Abraham, God required him and all the males in the household to be circumcised. This act of obedience symbolized the cutting away of sin and was an outward reminder of the covenant God made with His people.

Another covenant sign was when God saved Noah, his

family, and the animals from the flood. God set a rainbow in the clouds and declared that it would be the sign of the covenant between God and all the earth never again to send a flood to destroy all life. (Genesis 9:12-15) That is a beautiful sign that we still witness today.

A covenant is not just a nice promise; it is a serious oath, an agreement with a sign or a symbol that confirms it. A conditional covenant that requires obedience brings consequences for the people who disobey or disregard their part of the agreement. For an overview of the punishments of the Mosaic Covenant that would come to God's people if they did not obey God, read Deuteronomy 28:15-68. These are not just normal consequences for disobedience; these are curses from the hand of God that would be on the people God intended to bless but who chose to disobey God and live in rebellion against Him.

THE BLESSINGS OF COVENANTS

The blessings of a covenant are immeasurably more than the usual or normal blessings of life. When Abraham was 100 years old, he and Sarah miraculously had the baby that God had promised years earlier. Their child went on to produce generations of descendants that were promised by God in His covenant with Abraham.

The blessings of the Old Covenant were so much more than what God's people could bring upon themselves, no matter how hard they tried. The blessings listed in Deuteronomy 28:1-14 would come directly from the hand of God. He said the people would be blessed, established as His holy people, live in abundant prosperity, and defeat their enemies.

Most of all, the Old Covenant would point to the New

Covenant of Grace. Christians experience the blessings from the New Covenant today. We are saved by the grace of God and given the Holy Spirit to lead and guide us through life. We have the blessing of spiritual gifts so that we can serve the Lord and further His Kingdom here on earth. We have the blessing of joy, peace, and hope. We have the blessing of God who loves us, watches over us, intervenes for us, and hears our prayers.

What are the consequences of refusing the offer of the Covenant of Grace? Those who reject the grace of God will:

- ✦ ...continue to live a life of sin and experience sin's consequences
- ✦ ...not receive forgiveness from God
- ✦ ...not have the Holy Spirit to help counsel and guide them
- ✦ ...lose the opportunity to live their life's purpose for which they were created
- ✦ ...spend eternity in Hell which was meant for Satan and demons
- ✦ ...spend an eternity with all the others who chose rebellion over God
- ✦ ...spend eternity separated from God

The requirement to become part of the Covenant of Grace is faith in the Lord Jesus. Grace is the free, undeserved favor of the Lord. Grace is an amazing gift!

CHAPTER 11

God's Chosen People

About 2,000 years before Christ was born, God decided to have a special relationship with one specific people group, who later became known as the Hebrew, or Jewish, people. He chose to reveal Himself to individuals who would become a nation through whom He would bless the entire world. And one of the major themes of the Bible is the relationship between God and His chosen people.

It all started with Abram. Genesis 12 tells us that God spoke to Abram (his name was later changed to Abraham). He told Abram to go away from his country to a land that God would later show him. Thus began the relationship between God and the patriarch of the future nation of Israel.

This is what God said:

> "I will make you into a great nation, and I will bless you; I will make your name great and you will be a blessing. I will bless those who bless you, and whoever curses you I will curse; and all peoples on earth will be blessed through you." (Genesis 12:2-3)

Abram faithfully obeyed, packed up his possessions, left his homeland, and headed toward Canaan. The Lord spoke to Abram again,

> *"To your offspring I will give this land."*
> *(Genesis 12:7)*

God gave Abram a wonderful promise. The only problem was that he and his wife could not conceive. They waited many years for God's promise to be fulfilled. In Genesis 17:5, God changed Abram's name to Abraham when he was 99 years old to signify that he would be the father of many nations. Finally, God did a mighty miracle, just as He promised, and Abraham and Sarah had a baby boy named Isaac. By then, Abraham was 100 years old and Sarah was 90 years old!

Why would God choose Abraham to start a "great nation" through whom "all peoples on earth will be blessed"? Why him?

I don't think anyone can answer the specific question of what God saw in Abraham and why He selected him to be the one to start His chosen nation. But as we study the life of Abraham, we learn that even though he wasn't perfect, he had strong faith and trusted the Lord. God saw something in Abraham that he could work with to bless others. Some say that God chose Abraham because he was a believer in God and lived righteously. Abraham had already chosen to be separated from the pagan beliefs of that time. Knowing Abraham's heart and the way he lived, God decided, "He's the one who will be the patriarch of my chosen people!"

A FAVORED NATION

God did indeed choose a group of people through which He would bless the entire world. Relationship is extremely important to God. His plan was to demonstrate who He is through His relationship with His chosen people. God chose a small and insignificant group of people to become the nation through whom He would glorify Himself.

When I hear people question why Israel is God's "favorite," I explain that God didn't choose them simply to be blessed, rather to *be a blessing* to other nations. Notice the phrase in Genesis 12:3,

> "all peoples on earth will be blessed through you."

Also, it's important to know that God doesn't have "favorites," but He does have "intimates." He chose a nation that He could develop an intimacy with so that others around the world would learn about what it's like to be in a relationship with God. Granting favor to His chosen people is not the same as arbitrarily choosing "favorites." God chose Israel for a purpose and has granted His favor upon that nation.

Not only has God worked with and through the nation of Israel since Abraham's time, but God's entire plan of redemption and the end times of the world revolve around God's chosen people. Revelation 21:4 says:

> "He will wipe every tear from their eyes. There will be no more death or mourning or crying or pain, for the old order of things has passed away."

Verse 2 tells us that the victory will take place in Jerusalem.

BLESSINGS POURED OUT THROUGH GOD'S CHOSEN PEOPLE

Even though the Jewish people did not recognize Jesus as their Messiah, God has continued to fulfill His promise that this particular people group will be a blessing to all the nations. If you wonder how they have been a blessing to the world, here are some examples:

The long awaited and anticipated Messiah was prophesied in the Jewish Scriptures over 750 years prior to His birth.

PART 2: THE THEMES OF THE BIBLE

Our Lord and Savior, Jesus Christ, was born into a Jewish family and is of Jewish heritage. The Savior of the world came from God's chosen people.

Jesus has blessed the entire world by sacrificing His life and shedding His blood on the cross as payment for the sins of the world.

The Disciples were Jewish, followed Jesus, and learned from Him. All the Disciples (except Judas, who betrayed Jesus) spread the Gospel and began the Christian church.

The Apostle Paul, raised as a Jew, was personally called by the Lord Jesus to preach to the Gentiles. Paul wrote 13 books of the New Testament, which you and I rely on to learn specific doctrines of Christianity.

Our in-depth study of the Jewish documents in the Old Testament, including the prophets, the Psalms, and the history of God's people, teaches us about God, His characteristics, His faithfulness, and so much more. The written message of God to all of mankind has come through the history and prophets of God's chosen people.

The Apostle John (Jesus' most intimate Disciple) wrote the book of Revelation. The information in this book was revealed to him by Jesus and tells us specifically what will take place at the second coming of Jesus. Christians look forward to this extraordinary event with anticipation.

Jesus has promised to return, and will come to the Mount of Olives, which is just east of Jerusalem.

Nations who bless Israel have been blessed; God is keeping His word. Nations who curse Israel are and will be cursed.

Oh yes, our lives have been powerfully impacted by the writings, the lives, and the Messiah of God's chosen people.

I personally have been immensely blessed by God's

chosen people. I've studied their records, their stories, their history, and their prophets. Their Messiah has become my Savior. The Bible is my treasured possession. Through the Word of God, I've come to know the Lord in a very personal way. I have been so blessed by the fact that God chose to work through a group of people rather than simply shout from Heaven who He is and what's on His mind.

DO YOU WANT TO BE PART OF GOD'S CHOSEN PEOPLE?

The Bible tells us that the Jewish people are God's *treasured possession*.

> "For the Lord has chosen Jacob to be his own, Israel to be his treasured possession." (Psalm 135:4)

What a blessing, what a special relationship!

When people question why God chose Israel, some may even feel resentment that He made such a choice. Why them? Why not another people group? Why not my people? Those who ask such questions may forget that the chosen people of God have also received much persecution over the centuries. Along with the blessing of belonging to God as His treasured possession, this special group of people has suffered intensely over the centuries. In many cases, it has been clear that God's chosen people have been targeted by Satan himself. Certainly, they have been marked for destruction by many evil people over the course of history.

Here are some examples of persecution of Jewish people over the centuries:

When the Jews were enslaved in Egypt and their population was growing, Pharoah ordered Hebrew baby boys to be killed when they were born.

In ancient times the Jewish people were taken into captivity by the Babylonians and the Assyrians.

A law was passed in Persia that decreed the annihilation of all the Jews living in the land. You can read about how the Jews were spared in the Old Testament book of Esther.

When Jesus was born, wise men came from a far land and followed a star, a sign that the King of the Jews had been born. When King Herod learned of this, he had all baby boys under the age of two murdered, with the intent to kill the baby who was prophesied. That is why an angel told Mary and Joseph to take the baby Jesus to flee Bethlehem and escape to Egypt.

The Jewish people were persecuted by the Romans because their worship of one God was seen as rebellion against Caesar.

The Jews have experienced antisemitism in many ways over the centuries. In more recent history, over six million Jews were murdered under Hitler and the Nazi regime during World War II.

Satan has instilled a hatred in some people for God's chosen nation for thousands of years, with the goal of destroying God's treasured possession.

NOW, DO YOU *REALLY* WANT TO BE A PART OF GOD'S CHOSEN PEOPLE?

I have good news and bad news for you. If you are a Believer in Christ, the good news is that you are part of God's chosen people! Even in ancient times, those who believed in the God of Israel came under the same blessing of the Jews. Some Gentiles worshipped God, and although they weren't actually Jewish, they were allowed to partake, for example, in the Passover.

If a believing Gentile was circumcised, he could partake in the blessing of the Jews. He had to go through a permanent transformation, something that couldn't be undone, a physical mark that proved his belief.

> *"An alien living among you who wants to celebrate the Lord's Passover must have all the males in his household circumcised; then he may take part like one born in the land. No uncircumcised male may eat of it." (Exodus 12:48)*

The Apostle Paul refers to this in Colossians 2:11,

> *"In him you were also circumcised, in the putting off of the sinful nature, not with a circumcision done by the hands of men but with the circumcision done by Christ."*

This verse holds a deep spiritual truth that correlates with the Old Testament physical example of circumcision. If you are a true Believer in Christ, then you have also become God's treasured possession. You have experienced a spiritual circumcision of the heart, a permanent cutting away of sin, a mark that proves you are forgiven and are now in the family of God. God's family includes Believing Jews and Believing Gentiles.

Now for the bad news. Believers not only share in blessings from God, but they also share in the persecution that comes from those who hate God's people. Christians have suffered persecution and martyrdom since the Church began. Satan, in his hatred for Jesus, influences evil people to persecute those who follow the Lord. Around the world, even to this day, Christians are subject to persecution, suffering, and martyrdom for their faith. Jesus told His Disciples in John

15:20 that they would be persecuted, just as He was. As Jesus warned His followers that this would take place, He also said in John 16:33 that they should "take heart" because He has overcome the world.

GOD'S FAITHFULNESS TO ISRAEL

Has God forsaken His chosen people due to unbelief? Certainly not! God will prove His steadfast love and everlasting faithfulness to the nation that He chose as His own. God will manifest His blessings on the earth through the nation of Israel. The whole earth will witness the fullness of God's plan for His chosen nation. The physical manifestation of God's promises to His chosen people will unfold as promised. In the meantime, Believers continue to come into a relationship with the Messiah, the Lord Jesus. You and I share in the blessings of God's treasured possession.

CHAPTER 12

Reconciliation with God

The theme of reconciliation with God is one of the most important themes that runs throughout the pages of Scripture.

If you read the entire Bible, you will come to understand that God's message to mankind is reconciliation. The books of the Bible come together as one grand invitation, an appeal to all people:

"Come, be reconciled to God, the price for your sins has been paid, you are forgiven, repent and be reconciled!"

Why do we need to be reconciled with God? Why doesn't He just come to us, forgive us, and make everything right, like it was in the Garden of Eden?

Good questions!

If you desire immediate reconciliation, are you willing to throw away justice? If someone enters a school and kills students, why don't the authorities simply reconcile with the killer, forgive him and tell him to go on his way? We don't ignore crimes because of an important factor called *justice*. Letting someone go doesn't fix the sin problem. There must be payment and atonement in order for justice to be satisfied.

Our relationship with God became broken in the Garden of Eden. Adam and Eve placed their wills above God's will. They made a choice that broke the intimate fellowship that they once shared with their Creator. When people question the significance of one simple bite of a piece of fruit, they must realize that one bite was in defiance of God's Word. It proved their desire to rule their own lives, apart from God, and demonstrated doubt and unbelief in what God had said. The consequences of their choice still permeate the world and their descendants, even to this day. Because all people are born of Adam and Eve, everyone has inherited their sinful human nature.

It is amazing that immediately after Adam and Eve sinned, God already had a desire to reconcile and restore their relationship. Genesis 3:21 tells us that God made garments of skin for clothes for Adam and Eve. There had been no death up until that point. After they sinned, Adam and Eve hid from God because they were naked and ashamed. Then God shed the innocent blood of an animal to provide a covering for them.

The sacrificial system of the Jewish religion required the shedding of the blood of an animal for forgiveness of sins. Leviticus 4:3 and Exodus 12:5 tell us that the animal was required to be spotless, without defect, in other words, a "righteous, perfect" substitute. Someone, something else had to endure the punishment that was deserved. Instead of striking each and every person dead, forcing them to immediately pay for their sin, God accepted the blood of a substitute. An innocent, perfect lamb who did nothing wrong would pay the price.

God loves the masterpiece of His creation and provided reconciliation through the shedding of innocent blood. The blood of Jesus shed at Calvary provided the once and for all atonement and payment for the sins of the world. Jesus was our righteous, perfect substitute. Jesus, the spotless Lamb, provided a way to be reconciled with God. But what a price He paid on the cross! Jesus endured the shame, flogging, insults, curses, nails, darkness, and the full wrath of God as He hung on the cross. God poured out His wrath on Jesus for the sins of the world and accepted His shed blood as payment for our sins.

Reconciliation. Readers of God's Word will not miss this theme as they study the Scriptures. All those who place their faith in the Savior will be reconciled to God!

CHAPTER 13

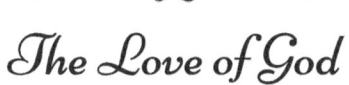

The Love of God

One of the messages we clearly see in the Bible is how much God loves us. "Us" means you and me and all of the other people in the world, for all time. The love of God is the foundation, the basis, and the reason that we have the Bible. God's love motivates Him to reconcile with the masterpiece of His creation. God's message throughout the Bible is reconciliation with God *because* of His great love for us.

Many people struggle with the idea that God loves them. Why? Because they don't "feel" His love. Their definition of love is quite different than God's definition. Some people define love as a feel good feeling. They *feel* loved if they are blessed. They *feel* love if things are going their way. But when faced with a challenge or a trial or suffering, they *feel* abandoned by God and certainly not loved.

But God loves us with a faithful, loyal, steadfast, and unconditional love. The Hebrew people described God's love as *hesed* love. "Hesed" carries the Hebrew meaning of loyal, unfailing, and steadfast. It implies a stubborn type of love that doesn't give up. When we are in a relationship with the Lord, we experience His unfailing love. Unfailing means completely dependable, not failing or undependable like human love can be. God's love is a faithful love that we can rely on and trust.

Isaiah 54:10 says,

> *"'Though the mountains be shaken and the hills be removed, yet my unfailing love for you will not be shaken, nor my covenant of peace be removed,' says the Lord, who has compassion on you."*

GOD'S LOVE IN THE OLD TESTAMENT

Have you ever been in a relationship with someone who betrayed you and broke the intimacy that you had with that person? It causes tremendous heartbreak. I wonder how God felt after enjoying intimacy with the two people He had created, Adam and Eve, and they sinned against Him. They broke the intimacy and fellowship that they had with God. In fact, after they sinned, they hid themselves in guilt and shame. But God's love for them caused Him to seek them and provide a way for them to be reconciled with Him.

The Bible tells us that God is love (1 John 4:16). He seeks us, speaks through His Word, convicts our hearts of sin, pleads with us to repent, and invites us into a relationship with Him.

We see this throughout the Old Testament. God displayed his steadfast, hesed love for His people in so many ways:

- ✦ He miraculously freed them from slavery under the Egyptians.
- ✦ He cared for them in the wilderness, providing food and water to them.
- ✦ He gave the Ten Commandments to guide His people into righteous living.
- ✦ He sought personal relationships with people, caring for them individually.

- He conquered enemies whose goal was to destroy God's people.
- He spoke through the prophets to convict them of sin and wrongful living.
- He gave them the hope of a coming Messiah.

I've heard people comment that the God of the Old Testament is mean and caused wars. People feel angry when they read about the wars, the killing, and the abolishment of pagan nations. Nothing could be further from the truth. God did not go around killing off nations of good people just to help His chosen people. No, the nations that God told His people to dispossess were nations that practiced idolatry and murder, and had no sense of humanity or righteousness. In those days, many nations were continuously at war with each other to gain land and power and turn populations of people into slaves. When nations captured people, they treated them inhumanely.

Each enemy nation had their own pagan god or multiple gods. Their spiritual acts of worship included prostitutes within their temples and child sacrifice through the fire. Their actions and beliefs and lifestyles were evil and a stench to God.

There is no record of God turning away from people who seek Him and love Him and want to be in a relationship with Him. When we read about God's judgment on people, it is due to their actions and their sin.

Mankind is sinful and God is love. This is what we learn when we study the Bible. God loves us and people continuously reject God and make sinful, hurtful, and hateful choices. God's love is demonstrated in the Old Testament by His faithful love toward His people. God is long suffering, slow to anger, and full of love.

> *"The Lord is compassionate and gracious, slow to anger, abounding in love." (Psalm 103:8)*

GOD'S LOVE IN THE NEW TESTAMENT

There is one sentence in the New Testament that sums up God's love for us. You may have memorized this verse when you were a child. It is the Gospel, the invitation, the display of God's love:

> *"For God so loved the world that he gave his one and only Son, that whoever believes in him shall not perish but have eternal life." (John 3:16)*

The invitation is, "...whoever believes in him...."

God's willingness to give His Son, watch Him suffer and die on the cross, is the evidence of His love for us. Don't think that because He is God that His heart wasn't filled with grief. Do not believe that because Jesus is God in flesh that His heart wasn't broken. Luke 22:44 tells us the extent of Jesus' sorrow in the Garden of Gethsemane. His sweat fell like drops of blood because of the extent of His anguish. How much love must God have for us to endure this traumatic event to be reconciled to us?

Jesus paid the highest price to redeem those who repent and believe in Him. Hebrews 12:2b tells us,

> *"...for the joy set before him, he endured the cross, scorning its shame, and sat down at the right hand of the throne of God."*

What was the joy that awaited Jesus after the resurrection? **The finished work of atonement** – The final and complete payment for the sins of the world, satisfying the wrath of God and judgment for sin.

The redemption of Believers – Jesus made a way for those who place their faith in Him to be reconciled to God and have everlasting life.

The creation of His Church – Jesus would build His Church and "the gates of Hades (Hell) will not overcome it." (Matthew 16:18)

The sending of the promised Holy Spirit to indwell and seal Believers – Jesus promised to send the Holy Spirit to indwell, help, comfort, guide, and seal Believers for eternity.

The bride of Christ – Jesus' love for His Church is compared to a groom that loves his bride. The bride of Christ (His Church) anticipates with joy the day of the wedding when Christ is united with His Church. (Revelation 19:7)

The victory over Satan – In His death and resurrection Jesus will triumph over Satan. (Colossians 2:15) In the end times Jesus will be victorious over sin and evil forever. (Revelation chapter 20)

God loves us, whether or not we accept it or feel it or experience it in the ways we expect. God's love is steadfast, faithful, and true. God draws us to Him by the work of the Holy Spirit, the Scriptures, and the Gospel of Jesus. The Holy Spirit works powerfully through the Gospel message and the Word of God to convict us of sin and invite us into a relationship with Him. Have you accepted the invitation and received the gift of salvation?

> *"I have loved you with an everlasting love; I have drawn you with loving-kindness." (Jeremiah 31:3b)*

CHAPTER 14

Reversal of Destiny

This is one of those beautiful themes in the Bible that helps us to understand that God is in control. Trusting God gives us hope when things seem to be going terribly wrong. There are times when God steps in and turns a person, circumstance, or event around. Suddenly, it all begins going in another direction. We read over and over in the Bible about how God turns things around for His people. Reversal of destiny is a good way to describe God's intervention when He turns a situation upside down, flips it over, reverses its course, and changes the destiny of people.

A wonderful example is the story of Esther, the beautiful Jewish girl who was chosen to marry the king and become the queen of Persia. A Persian official named Haman convinced the king to sign a law that decreed the destruction of all the Jewish people. Because Queen Esther was willing to risk her life to plead to the king on behalf of her people, the direction of the circumstances turned completely around. God's people were saved from annihilation, and Haman was hung on the very gallows that he built to kill an innocent Jewish man named Mordecai (Esther's cousin). God performed a miracle and set things right for the good of His people. Though God is not mentioned in this book, His presence is evident and He was in control of the outcome.

Another reversal of destiny example is when Joseph was languishing in prison after being falsely accused. His story is told in Genesis chapters 37-50. Joseph was sold into slavery by his own brothers. While serving in his master's house, he was falsely accused and thrown into prison for years. Life was going in a hopeless direction for Joseph. But God had a plan all along and worked out Joseph's circumstances to accomplish God's greater purpose. In one day, Joseph was released from prison and sent before Pharoah to interpret his dream. That same day, an amazed and grateful Pharoah promoted Joseph to become second in command over the whole kingdom. Joseph's high position in Egypt enabled him to save his family, which was the future nation of Israel, from famine. Now that's a reversal of destiny!

God is able to turn things around because He is all powerful. The story of Jabez in 1 Chronicles 4:9-10 tells us that Jabez' mother was in great pain when she gave birth to him. She named him Jabez which means "pain." Maybe his mom expected that he would live a life of pain. But Jabez wanted God to change that prediction of his future. He cried out to the Lord and prayed,

> *"Oh, that you would bless me and enlarge my territory! Let your hand be with me, and keep me from harm so that I will be free from pain."*
> *(verse 10)*

At the end of that verse we read,

> *"And God granted his request."*

Reversal of destiny. Oh, how God loves to turn things in a new direction!

Reversal of Destiny

The ultimate "But God" moment

As you read the Bible, you can watch for the times when God suddenly intervenes and turns things around for His people. Even Isaiah wrote what God said about this very topic:

> *"I foretold the former things long ago, my mouth announced them and I made them known; then suddenly I acted, and they came to pass."*
> *(Isaiah 48:3)*

When you see the words "but God" in the Bible, that is a clue that God is in control and He will act in the situation. I love reading about the "but God" events as I study the Scriptures. Even if you haven't read the Bible, you have most likely heard about the most powerful "but God" event that our world has ever known.

It started with the crucifixion of Jesus. Criminal treatment and punishment were inflicted upon the sinless Son of God. All hope seemed to disappear as Jesus hung on the cross. *Wasn't He the Messiah? Didn't He do miracles? Why is this happening? What are we going to do?*

Oh, what dark and hopeless few days those must have been for the Disciples and followers of Jesus. Darkness, confusion, anguish, hopelessness.

But God...

On the third day after the crucifixion, when Mary and the women went to the tomb to anoint Jesus' body, they heard the words that changed the world.

> *"You are looking for Jesus the Nazarene, who was crucified. He has risen! He is not here." (Mark 16:6)*

Wow! This reversal of destiny changed everything. Jesus

rose from the grave! He overcame our greatest enemy, death. Jesus opened the way for us to go to Heaven.

OUR PERSONAL "REVERSAL OF DESTINY"

If you are a Christian, you are living proof of the principle of "reversal of destiny." You were heading in one direction, a life of sin, separated from God, with no hope of Heaven.

> *"For the wages of sin is death, but the gift of God is eternal life in Christ Jesus our Lord." (Romans 6:23)*

You were headed for death which is permanent separation from God. That was your direction and destiny. Then, someone told you about Jesus, or you went to church and heard a sermon, or you read the Bible, or something happened that caused you to realize that you were lost. You repented and turned away from sin and believed. You trusted the Lord Jesus and received the gift of the Holy Spirit. *Little did you know that you experienced the most magnificent reversal of destiny!*

My reversal of destiny happened while I was looking at a piece of paper with the address of a Bible Study. I had just left the church office after talking with one of the pastors. I told him I was unhappy and couldn't figure out why. I was in my 20's and after years of ignoring God, I started going back to church, but my life hadn't changed. Every weekend I was still doing the same worldly activities I did during college, then I would go to church on Sunday. The pastor said it was very simple; I was living with one foot in the world and one foot with the Lord. I needed to make a choice.

As I sat in my car in the parking lot outside of the church office, I made my choice as I looked at the piece of paper the pastor gave me. *Well, if it's that simple, I choose Jesus!*

Instead of going out as usual with my friends, I went to the Bible Study at the address on the piece of paper. When I arrived there was a group of young people who were laughing and having fun. There were two guys playing guitars and singing. I was introduced and visited with them for a while, then we spent time talking about the Bible.

I'll never forget my thought as I entered that room of young Christians: *This is my new life, I'm never going back!*

That reversal of direction for me became my reversal of destiny.

Has your destiny been reversed yet?

CHAPTER 15

The Names of God

In our society, names are legal identities. If we want to officially change our name, we must go through the court system to accomplish it. Surely names also represent reputation. That's why many people don't name their children after someone who has committed a terrible crime or someone who was an evil dictator. It takes a long time to build a good reputation and our name represents us. Proverbs 22:1 tells us,

> *"A good name is more desirable than great riches; to be esteemed is better than silver or gold."*

Are we careful not to defile a person's name? Spreading false information about someone is gossip and slander. Ruining a person's reputation has lasting effects that could impact an entire family. How many fights have taken place over the centuries in order to defend the family name?

The culture of God's people in the Bible placed a very high importance on names. Names identified families and where they came from. Names were recorded very carefully and thoroughly. A newborn's name was connected to the destiny of the child. The name was carefully chosen based on the qualities the baby was expected to have or the characteristics that the parents hoped would develop.

Part 2: The Themes of the Bible

We learn from the Bible that God changed the names of several people. He had good reason to do that as He was leading the person in a new direction in life. Each individual had a new purpose and God wanted their new names to reflect that. Here are some examples:

- Abram – God changed his name to Abraham to indicate God's plan for Abram which was to become "father of many nations." (Genesis 17:5)
- Jacob – God changed his name to Israel because he had "struggled with God and with men and had overcome." (Genesis 32:28)
- Simon – Jesus changed Simon's name to Peter which means "rock." (John 1:42) Peter's powerful declaration of the truth of Jesus was to be the rock on which Jesus would build His Church.

The importance of God's names

God has many names that describe His character and what He is able to do. Each of God's names tells us more about the God we serve.

Here are some of the names of God in the Bible:

- Jehovah Jireh – "The Lord will provide" (Genesis 22:14)
- Jehovah Rapha – "The God that heals" (Exodus 15:26)
- Jehovah Nissi – "The Lord is my banner" (Exodus 17:15)
- Jehovah Rohi – "The Lord is my Shepherd" (Psalm 23)
- Jehovah Shalom – "The Lord is Peace" (Judges 6:24)
- Yahweh – "LORD" or "Jehovah" or "I AM"

(Exodus 3:13-15) (When you see LORD in all capital letters in the Bible, that is the English translation of Yahweh.)

The name of God represents His righteousness and His power. Proverbs 18:10 says,

> *"The name of the Lord is a strong tower; the righteous run to it and are safe."*

Not only do we run to the strong tower of God's name when we're in trouble, but the Bible tells us that God's name is to be praised all day long.

> *"From the rising of the sun to the place where it sets, the name of the Lord is to be praised." (Psalm 113:3)*

We are to praise God's name, defend His name, and proclaim His name. David, the shepherd boy who became King of Israel, did exactly that when he fought the giant, Goliath. He was so angered by Goliath, the representative of the Philistine army who was "defying the armies of the living God," that David was willing to risk his own life to protect God's Holy Name. Here is what David said before slinging a stone into the forehead of this giant,

> *"...You come against me with sword and spear and javelin, but I come against you in the name of the Lord Almighty, the God of the armies of Israel, whom you have defied." (1 Samuel 17:45)*

David, the young shepherd boy with only a slingshot, killed the nine-foot giant who was covered with armor, spear, and shield. How did David accomplish this? God enabled David to win the battle because of his faith and desire to honor God and defend His name.

PART 2: THE THEMES OF THE BIBLE

THE REVERENCE FOR GOD'S NAMES

When Jesus spoke the Lord's prayer, the first sentence He said was:

> *"Our Father in heaven, hallowed be your name...."*
> *(Matthew 6:9a)*

Hallowed means holy. What does holy mean? Something that is pure, perfect, set apart. Someone who is sacred, sinless, exalted, and deserves our worship.

God spoke to Moses at the burning bush in Exodus chapter 3. He instructed Moses to go to Pharoah to bring God's people out of Egypt. Moses asked God his name so that he could tell the people who sent him. Verse 14 tells us,

> *"God said to Moses, I AM WHO I AM. This is what you are to say to the Israelites: 'I AM has sent me to you.'"*

Remember this name of God, "I AM." You will encounter it again in the New Testament when Jesus boldly stated in John 8:58,

> *"I tell you the truth... before Abraham was born, I am!"*

The people who heard this knew that Jesus was calling Himself the very name of God, making Himself equal to God. For this reason, they tried to stone Him, but He slipped away in the crowd.

The Jewish people held such reverence for the name "Yahweh" or "I Am" that they would not even speak the word. Why did they revere the name so intensely? Reverencing God's name is so important that God included it in the Ten Commandments. The Jewish people feared that they might inadvertently break the commandment to not take the Lord's name in vain. In order to protect themselves, they did not say the name of the Lord.

MISUSE OF GOD'S NAME

Not only does God command that we do not take His name in vain, but the Bible also says that if we do this, we will be punished. Our casual misuse of His Holy Name will not go unnoticed. It will not be ignored. It will not be brushed off as a slip of the tongue or an accidental profanity.

> *"You shall not misuse the name of the Lord your God, for the Lord will not hold anyone guiltless who misuses his name." (Exodus 20:7)*

The Levitical Law condemned the blasphemer of God's name to death. Leviticus 24:16 says:

> *"...anyone who blasphemes the name of the Lord is to be put to death. The entire assembly must stone him. Whether alien or native-born, when he blasphemes the Name, he must be put to death."*

Blaspheming God's name is to speak with utter disrespect to the Holiness of God. There is so much power in His name and it represents all that God is. To blaspheme God's name is to hate God and hate all that He is. The punishment for blasphemy in the Old Testament Law was very serious. It was death by stoning. If we think the punishment doesn't fit the crime, then we should consider why it was so important to God. Why would God be so angry with blasphemy of His name? Our meager human speculation doesn't even reach the depths of God's true perspective on this matter.

Although the punishment for misuse of God's name today

doesn't seem to carry any penalty, it was important enough to God to make it one of the Ten Commandments. (Exodus 20:7, Deuteronomy 5:11) It is the evidence of a heart that rebels against God. Just as your name and reputation matter to you, how much more does the Holiness of God matter to Him?

How do people misuse the name of God?

Using God's name in vain is speaking or using His name in a way that does not accurately reflect God's character. Here are ways that God's name is used in vain:

Using God's name as profanity. This is the opposite of respecting and reverencing God's name. To be so frivolous with the most powerful name is rebellious and sinful. People who don't know God and don't understand His character and power find it easy to use God's name casually, even as a curse word.

Associating God's name with a wrong doctrine or false information about God. People misuse God's name by stating false beliefs about God. False doctrines and man-made belief systems are common ways that people disrespect God and use His name in vain. It is serious to use God's name to falsely describe His character. It creates a barrier to faith and may cause a person not to believe in God. Salvation is at stake if people are driven away from God because they believed lies about Him.

Attributing to someone else what God has authored. The Pharisees (teachers of the Law) did this when they gave credit to Satan for miracles that Jesus had done. They claimed that Jesus did not do the miracles by the power of God, rather by "Beelzebub, the prince of demons." (Matthew 12:24). To witness a marvelous miracle of God, yet attribute it to the devil, is another way of disrespecting the name of God.

Attributing to or blaming God for something He has not authored. There are people who believe that all things come by the hand of God, including sin and evil. This is another way that people wrongly use God's name. Attributing to God something that is authored by Satan is falsely representing God. The Bible clearly teaches that God is not the author of sin. We must be careful not to blame God for the work of Satan, the sin of mankind, or our own personal sin.

Our God is so holy, so compassionate, and loves us so much that He will not tolerate the blatant rebellion of something so basic as reverence for His name. We must worship and revere God Himself, but if we do not honor His name, that is surely the foremost sign of overt disrespect and lack of reverence.

THE NAME ABOVE ALL NAMES

Now, let's look at the Name above all names. The Name that is so powerful and so holy that if you want to be saved and go to Heaven for eternity, you only get there through the power of this Name!

JESUS

Why is the name of Jesus "above" all names? The Bible tells us in Philippians 2:9-11,

> *"Therefore God exalted him to the highest place and gave him the name that is above every name, that at the name of Jesus every knee should bow, in heaven and on earth and under the earth, and every tongue confess that Jesus Christ is Lord, to the glory of God the Father."*

Every tongue will confess that Jesus is Lord? Yes, and that means both Believers and unbelievers. No one will escape the moment of facing the Lord Jesus and the recognition that He is exalted to the highest place. All people will face Jesus, bow their knees to Him, and acknowledge that He is Lord.

I would rather meet the Lord having believed and honored His name than to cringe in shame upon facing Jesus, thinking, *"Jesus is Lord! How could I have ignored this truth?"*

Not only is the name of Jesus higher than all names, but the power of His name is explained in Acts 4:12:

> *"Salvation is found in no one else, for there is no other name under heaven given to men by which we must be saved."*

In fact, Romans 10:13 is a powerful verse in the Bible that is actually a promise to all of us regarding the name of Jesus:

> *"Everyone who calls on the name of the Lord will be saved."*

Think about that verse. Everyone? Yes, everyone. What does it mean to call on the name of the Lord? It means that everyone who calls to the Lord Jesus in faith and believes in Him will be saved.

Here are a few other names of Jesus that will help us understand the depth of His majesty and power:

- ✢ Son of Man
- ✢ Prince of Peace
- ✢ Savior
- ✢ Messiah
- ✢ Christ
- ✢ Mighty God
- ✢ Lamb of God

✦ Emmanuel

Finally, in the book of the Revelation, we read the description of John's vision of Jesus' return. Revelation 19:11 tells us that John saw Heaven open and there was a "white horse, whose rider is called Faithful and True." Jesus is going to return to earth! Faithful and True describe our Lord; He is faithful to everything He promises and all He says is true. Then John sees names of Jesus written on His robe as He rides into victory on a white horse. Revelation 19:16 tells us,

> *"On his robe and on his thigh he has this name written: KING OF KINGS AND LORD OF LORDS."*

PRAYING IN JESUS' NAME

The power, the majesty, and holiness of Jesus' name. The name above all names. And you and I have the blessing and the privilege to access and use the name of Jesus.

If someone knocked on your door and said you are invited to a ball at the White House, you might be tempted to think it was a joke. But if the messenger showed you proof that he is inviting you on behalf of or in the name of the President, you would take it more seriously. It would mean the same to you as if the President came to invite you in person. Why? Because the person has the authority to act on behalf of the President.

Using someone's name is very important. The name represents all that the person is. Because Jesus is the only way to the Father, we pray to God in Jesus' name. When we pray in Jesus' name, we are praying according to His will. We recognize the power of His name and so we end our prayers with "in Jesus' name, Amen." We are praying what Jesus would pray if He were standing right here. We pray according to what He wants above all.

We also are praying for the sake of Jesus. "For the sake of" means to pray for the cause or interest of Jesus. And so we pray and end our prayers with "In Jesus' name and for His sake" as we seek to further His will, His cause, and His interests here on earth.

It is a powerful thing to pray in Jesus' name. This is not to be taken lightly. We do not pray for our will to be done and hope that Jesus will give us His stamp of approval. No, we pray according to His will, and we expect His will to be done in the matter we are praying about. We will rejoice in His will being accomplished.

FAITHFUL TO HIS NAME

Would you like to be faithful to His name? We are not perfect, although as Believers we are in the sanctification process. Our journey on earth will always be a struggle. But we should persevere and continuously strive to be faithful to the Lord as we represent and honor His name.

There are some who say they believe and honor the name of Jesus yet do not live in obedience to Him. Jesus extends a warning to those who appear to honor His name but do not live according to God's will. Luke 6:46 says,

> *"Why do you call me, 'Lord, Lord,' and do not do what I say?"*

In Matthew 7:21 Jesus explains what happens to false followers:

> *"Not everyone who says to me 'Lord, Lord,' will enter the kingdom of heaven, but only the one who does the will of my Father who is in heaven."*

YAHWEH-SHALOM

The name of God is peace for you and me. Yahweh-Shalom or Jehovah-Shalom means *The Lord is Peace.* God is our source of peace.

Whatever we are going through, one of God's names represents something about His character that speaks to our lives. That's what I love about the names of God. Each name is truth about the one True God. Are you thirsty? Jesus is the Living Water. Are you spiritually hungry? Jesus is the Bread of Life. Are you anxious? God is the Lord of Peace.

As you read the Bible, notice the names of God. They signify and display the attributes of our God and Savior.

> *"Glorify the Lord with me; let us exalt his name together." (Psalm 34:3)*

CHAPTER 16

The Tabernacle, Temple, and Heaven

You might not have a great interest in reading about the tabernacle or the temple. *What does that have to do with me? Those are in the Old Testament and I can't relate!*

In reality, the tabernacle and the temple have everything to do with all Believers. The theme of the tabernacle and temple flows throughout Scripture, both Old and New Testaments.

THE TABERNACLE

After being freed from slavery under Egypt, the Israelites lived in the desert for 40 years. God instructed Moses to build a tabernacle, a place where God would dwell. The tabernacle was made of curtains over a wood frame and was mobile. As the Israelites traveled from place to place, they would dismantle the structure and rebuild it. You could think of the tabernacle as a temporary temple. It was more fragile than a building made of stone. But it served as the temple for the people. Inside was a room called the Holy of Holies, the place where God's presence would reside. The only item in the room was the Ark of the Covenant, which contained the tablets of the

Ten Commandments.

Only the High Priest was allowed in the Holy of Holies and only once a year to make atonement for the sins of the people. This Day of Atonement was so important that Yom Kippur is still celebrated today among the Jewish people.

Just think about how important the tabernacle must have been to the Israelites as they wandered through the desert. The presence of God was with them! Remember, they didn't have a Bible or a temple made of stone. They had one big tent, the tabernacle. That was it. There was much reverence for the tabernacle.

THE TEMPLE

Finally! The temple of stone, wood, gold, fine fabrics, and gems was built under King Solomon. It was an amazing and beautiful temple that would shout to the world, "Our God is worthy of such a marvelous place of worship!"

And what a temple it was. It was a glorious temple, built with cedar and stone, walls overlaid with gold and beautiful carvings on the interior. This was the place of worship for the Jews for about 400 years. That temple was destroyed in 586 B.C. when Jerusalem was sieged by King Nebuchadnezzar. A second temple was built about 70 years later and enlarged hundreds of years later under King Herod.

The temple was the place of worship and sacrifice, as the priests would perform the rituals, sacrifices, and other duties. Many Jewish people would travel for miles to come to Jerusalem several times a year to celebrate specific feasts and enjoy festivals.

The temple was destroyed by the Romans in 70 A.D. Matthew 24:2 records that Jesus had predicted this destruction.

The Bible reveals that there will be a third temple which will be built on the temple mount in the city of Jerusalem. (2 Thessalonians 2:4)

WHERE IS GOD'S DWELLING PLACE NOW?

The answer to that question is simple, yet very profound. God dwells in Heaven, but through the Holy Spirit, He resides, rules, and reigns in the hearts of Believers. Paul tells us in 1 Corinthians 6:19-20:

> *"Do you not know that your body is a temple of the Holy Spirit, who is in you, whom you have received from God? You are not your own, you were bought at a price. Therefore honor God with your body."*

Our bodies are the sacred dwelling place of God Himself. Jesus promised His followers,

> *"But I tell you the truth: It is for your good that I am going away. Unless I go away, the Counselor will not come to you; but if I go, I will send him to you." (John 16:7)*

Jesus sends the Holy Spirit to live inside of Believers. We become God's dwelling place!

It is quite amazing that God chooses to live inside of imperfect, sinful people. It is humbling and wondrous to know that when the Holy Spirit comes to live inside of Believers, He will be there forever, never to leave, always helping and guiding us. His indwelling is permanent and seals us for eternity in Heaven.

HEAVEN – THE TRUE AND ULTIMATE TEMPLE

We as Believers are blessed with the Holy Spirit living

inside of us. We don't have to go to a physical building to experience the presence of God, as in ancient times. If we would only appreciate the magnitude of such a blessing! God Himself lives in the hearts of His people.

Does this magnificent truth erase the importance of the physical temple of the Jewish people? Why bother studying the temple, its significance, the symbols and the pattern? Isn't that all unimportant now that we enjoy the spiritual fulfillment of the Holy of Holies?

We get a glimpse of Heaven as we study the details about the temple. If you notice the instructions that God gave to Moses for the tabernacle and Solomon for the temple, you might ask why God was so specific. Why did everything have to be so measured and perfect?

The tabernacle and the temple were very important because they point to Christ. They were constructed according to a specific pattern, which is actually a pattern of heavenly things. Hebrews 8:5 tells us that the sanctuary (the temple) is a copy and shadow of what is in Heaven. That is why Moses had to make everything according to the specific pattern that he was instructed to follow.

When we learn about the role of the High Priest, who made atonement for the sins of the people, we have a greater understanding of Jesus when He is called our "Great High Priest." Whereas the High Priest was required to continually make sacrifices for the forgiveness of the sins of the people, Jesus made a once and for all sacrifice by shedding His blood as atonement for our sins.

There are many other symbols in the temple that hold deep spiritual significance; in fact, everything within the temple held meaning. The temple is an image, a physical representation of something so much greater. It's a physical prototype of our future heavenly home.

Becoming familiar with the temple of the ancient Jewish people deepens our understanding of Jesus and our Christian faith. I was awestruck to learn that if you look at a diagram of the placement of the 12 tribes around the tabernacle, it is in the shape of a cross. In other words, from above, the tabernacle with God's people around it, situated in their correlating tribe locations, looks like a cross. Could it be that from God's vantage point, He saw the cross when His people were settled around the tabernacle?

There is so much symbolism that carries deep meaning for us as we open our hearts to learn about the tabernacle, the temple, and our future in Heaven. The map, the template, and the symbolism of the ancient tabernacle and temple point to Jesus our Savior!

PART 3

The Power of the Bible

CHAPTER 17

The Power of the Word of God

Have you ever felt the amazing power of the Word of God when you read passages in the Bible? Have you been comforted by the words on the pages of the Bible when you were so upset that no one could help you feel better? I have experienced moments when a verse seems to jump off the pages of Scripture and speak right to a problem I'm dealing with or something I have been worried about. My soul has been filled with fresh courage and stronger faith to overcome the challenging times in my life. After facing the confusion and messiness of the world, my mind has been renewed with hope, wisdom, and assurance after spending time in God's Word.

Is this all simply coincidental? Are these edifying and comforting moments simply the result of hearing some nice, helpful advice? Is the Bible just filled with a lot of positive, encouraging, self-help types of writings?

Or... is God's Word really so powerful, so alive, so filled with God Himself, that the very words on the pages actually minister to us, give us life, and purify us?

The Bible itself answers this question and tells us where its power comes from. After all, there is no higher authority than God's Word, so let's see what the Bible says about the Source of its power.

John chapter 1 is a good place to start when describing the power of God's Word. John 1:1 reveals that the "Word" is not like any other word. John begins his Gospel account with a powerful statement of truth about Jesus. "In the beginning was the Word, and the Word was with God, and the Word was God."

The Greek word used in the original text is "logos" which carries the meaning of expression or message. John is using the word "logos" as a title or a name for Jesus. John is telling us that Jesus is the Word and He existed before everything. He was with God and is God. Jesus is the full manifestation of God, the message of God, the expression of God, the logos. He is God.

> *"Anyone who has seen me has seen the Father."*
> *(John 14:9b)*

> *"I and the Father are one."*
> *(John 10:30)*

> *"'I tell you the truth,' Jesus answered, 'before Abraham was born, I am!'"*
> *(John 8:58)*

> *"For in Christ all the fullness of the Deity lives in bodily form."*
> *(Colossians 2:9)*

Jesus is the Word, the fullness of God, the expression, the mind of God, the very nature of God.

GOD'S WORD IS ALIVE

Hebrews 4:12 tells us that the Word of God is "alive and

active."

The Word of God is powerful because it is ***alive*** and ***active***. How can the words on the pages of Scripture be "alive" or "living"? John 1:14 tells us:

> *"The Word became flesh and made his dwelling among us."*

Jesus is the living Word of God. He is the fullness and the image of the living God. He is eternal. The Bible is God's message. And Jesus, being the living Word, is God's living message to mankind!

God's Word is alive and always working, even thousands of years after the words were written down. But how can the words on the pages of Scripture, or even the spoken words of God, contain power? The Holy Spirit takes the Word of God and works powerfully in the heart and mind of the person who has faith. The power of the Holy Spirit works through the words on the pages of Scripture, whether written, spoken, preached, read, sung, or however it is communicated. The very words of God are alive. The very Word of God is powerful!

Let's consider the Bible's self-description of its power:
- ✛ God's Word cuts us open like a knife, exposing the sin within us, and judges our thoughts and attitudes. (Hebrews 4:12)
- ✛ It is a hammer that can break open the hardest of hearts. (Jeremiah 23:29)
- ✛ It purges away the dross, the sin that poisons us. (Isaiah 1:25)
- ✛ The Bible gives us knowledge and understanding. (Proverbs 2:6)

- It is perfect, trustworthy, making us wise, giving light to our eyes. (Psalm 19:7-8)
- God's Word is the source of truth. (John 17:17)
- The Word of God is flawless. (Proverbs 30:5)
- It gives us joy. (Psalm 119:14, 1 John 1:4, Psalm 19:8)
- It renews our strength. (Isaiah 40:31)
- It guides us. (Psalm 119:105)
- It helps us grow. (1 Peter 2:2)
- The Bible prunes us, cutting off what inhibits full growth and potential. (John 15)
- When we hear and obey God's Word, it's like building a house on a strong foundation. (Luke 6:47-48)
- The Bible transforms us by renewing our minds. (Romans 12:2)
- The truth of the Bible unites Christians. (1 Corinthians 1:10)

God's Word is alive and never stops working within us as we continuously delve into Scripture. We are not reading passages that are empty of power; we are reading the living and active Word of God!

GOD SPEAKS TO US INDIVIDUALLY THROUGH HIS WORD

The Holy Spirit works through the words on the pages of the Bible to speak to us, convict our hearts, teach us, comfort us, minister to us, and much more.

The Holy Spirit will impress upon our hearts or convict us of specific truth when we read and study God's Word. As our lives move forward to new situations and circumstances change, we face new problems and challenges. Yet God's

Word ministers to us at the specific point of our need (over and over again)!

The Holy Spirit may use a passage to burn within you or break your heart open.

> *"'Is not my word like fire,' declares the Lord, 'and like a hammer that breaks a rock in pieces?'"*
> *(Jeremiah 23:29)*

We learn from the whole Word of God. But at times, the Lord speaks to us individually or says something very specific from His Word. In the Greek language, there are two words used to describe the Word of God. "Logos" refers to the whole Word of God and the record of His Word. "Rhema" means something more specific, words that are spoken or communicated. This term refers to the word spoken specifically to an individual. There are times when I read the Word of God (logos) and I have a strong sense that God is giving me a rhema (specific, custom word) from the logos. The rhema is God's personalized counsel for my specific need or situation.

How amazing that God speaks specifically to us as we seek Him through His Word. That is how the living, active, penetrating Word of God works in the lives of Believers who study the Bible.

So, how do we respond to this extraordinary book that exerts such power over its readers? We should desire it (more than gold or riches) and pursue it (as precious treasure).

What does it mean to pursue it?

SEEK

> *"You will seek me and find me when you seek me with all your heart." (Jeremiah 29:13)*

PART 3: THE POWER OF THE BIBLE

We seek the Lord through His written Word. We press on in the study of Scripture to come to know God. We pursue God with all the means that are available to us. We study the Bible, fellowship with other Believers, and attend a Bible-believing church. We keep our search for the Lord pure; in other words, we don't muddy our own path by filling our minds with rubbish from the world. We keep our eyes, ears, and activities pure and free from temptation and sinful choices.

BELIEVE

We don't reject or rebel against what God's Word teaches us. We believe. We know that it's true. We are careful that our belief doesn't end with a simple acknowledgement of the truth, rather making choices that match what we say we believe.

> *"I tell you the truth, whoever hears my word and believes him who sent me has eternal life and will not be condemned; he has crossed over from death to life." (John 5:24)*

> *"And we also thank God continually because, when you received the word of God, which you heard from us, you accepted it not as the word of men, but as it actually is, the word of God, which is at work in you who believe." (1 Thessalonians 2:13)*

PRAY

Prayer is one of the greatest gifts that God has given us. God has opened wide a direct line of communication for human beings to talk to the God of the universe. We have the privilege of being able to talk with God any time we want!

We can come to the Lord, not cowering in fear and shame, rather with confidence and hope. Hebrews 4:16 says,

> *"Let us then approach the throne of grace with confidence, so that we may receive mercy and find grace to help us in our time of need."*

When we pray, the Holy Spirit convicts us of sin in our lives. Oh yes, He will remind us that we are going before a Holy God and we need to repent of our sin. When we repent, we are cleansed as we approach the "throne of grace."

We should pray about everything! Philippians 4:6 tells us,

> *"Do not be anxious about anything, but in everything, by prayer and petition, with thanksgiving, present your requests to God."*

HIDE GOD'S WORD IN OUR HEARTS

> *"I have hidden your word in my heart that I might not sin against you." (Psalm 119:11)*

We study Scripture daily, learning it so that it becomes part of us. We memorize Scripture and "hide" verses in our hearts. We rely on the Bible to guide our ways throughout our daily lives so that we don't stray into sin.

OBEY

> *"Why do you call me 'Lord, Lord,' and do not do what I say?" (Luke 6:46)*

Pursuing God's Word means to strive and chase after, being intent to follow it. How can we call Jesus "Lord" yet turn from Him and disobey what He says? We must obey what we learn and conform our lives to the Word of God. "Conform" means to yield or to harmonize ourselves with the truth.

REJOICE IN GOD'S WORD

We rejoice because we have God's Word. We rejoice because the Scriptures guide us so that we don't stumble into sin.

Psalm 119, the longest chapter in the Bible, is all about the Word of God, the Law, the commandments, and the precepts of Scripture. The writer praises God for His Word and goes into great detail about how he is blessed by it:

> *"I rejoice in following your statutes as one rejoices in great riches." (vs. 14)*

> *"Direct me in the path of your commands, for there I find delight." (vs. 35)*

> *"I delight in your commands because I love them." (vs. 47)*

> *"Let your compassion come to me that I may live, for your law is my delight." (vs. 77)*

> *"Oh, how I love your law! I meditate on it all day long." (vs. 97)*

HE WHO HAS EARS TO HEAR

Jesus plainly explained to His listeners in Matthew 7:24-27 that everyone who hears His words and puts them into practice will be like a wise man building a house on a rock. No storm will make the house fall. But He warned those who hear His words and choose not to put them into practice. He said they are like a foolish man who built a house on sand. When the storm came, it fell with a "great crash."

Hearing is a choice. The person who believes in God, wants to learn, and obeys what he does learn is like the first man in His example. His life ("house") will be on the foundation that can withstand any storm. But the person who hears and decides to reject, rebel, and live in disobedience to God's Word will find his life falling apart when storms and winds blow through his life.

When I was in college, I tried to read the Bible. I hadn't attended church in a few years and was living my life my own way. I wasn't truly seeking the Lord, but just thought I'd read the Bible. The words on the pages didn't make much sense, there wasn't anything that seemed to speak to me or touch my heart or make me more interested. The words felt far away and meaningless.

Several years later, when I committed my life to the Lord and turned away from the choices I had been making, I began reading the Bible again. Immediately the words came alive to me. My soul was filled and refreshed every time I read the pages. I understood what I was reading and studying. It was like the veil had been pulled away from my heart and mind.

This is just a small personal example of how the Holy Spirit opens our minds and hearts to the Word of God. What was the change that helped me to experience the power of God's Word? The key to understanding the truth of Scripture is the Holy Spirit. Will the Holy Spirit open the mind of a person who deliberately rejects the truth by continuing to indulge in sin?

1 Corinthians 2:10-14 tells us that no one understands the thoughts of God except the Spirit of God. And we cannot

understand God without the Spirit. Verse 14 says,

> *"The man without the Spirit does not accept the things that come from the Spirit of God, for they are foolishness to him and he cannot understand them, because they are spiritually discerned."*

Friend, if you don't understand what you are reading in Scripture, pray that the Holy Spirit will open your heart and mind to the Word of God. But first, answer the simple question: Am I willing to confess my sin and begin a life of obedience to the Lord? Your humility and willingness are the response God desires in order for you to hear His message to you.

> *"This is the one I esteem: he who is humble and contrite in spirit, and trembles at my word."*
> *(Isaiah 66:2b)*

To tremble at God's Word doesn't mean approaching the Bible with fear, rather reverence and awe. We should be in awe of God's Word and its power.

CONTEND FOR THE WORD OF GOD

The Bible is powerful enough to teach us God's mind and change our lives, but it doesn't stop there. Hearers and doers of the Word of God are to contend for the Bible in our society and culture. To contend means to strive for the Word of God, determined to make the truth known.

And as we learn the Bible, we should defend God's Word in our sphere of influence. Defending God's Word means standing up for it and proving its validity. We should not be silent among the many people who live in ignorance regarding the Word of God. We should be able to defend the Bible as the true, infallible, revelation of the Creator of the universe, who offers forgiveness for our sin and eternal life in Heaven.

We should share our knowledge of the truth of the Bible wherever God lead us so that others can be blessed and transformed by the Word of God.

CHAPTER 18

Sharper than a Two-edged Sword

The writer of the book of Hebrews describes the Word of God as "sharper than any double-edged sword." (Hebrews 4:12) Why would the Bible be described as something like a sword?

A sword is sharp, it cuts, and it needs to be handled carefully. It's a powerful weapon. It penetrates deeply, cutting through everything in its way, opening and exposing what is hidden.

In reality, that is an accurate description of the Word of God!

The Bible pierces our hearts, cuts us open, and penetrates even to the deepest part of our soul. It convicts us of sin, exposes the deepest part of us, and opens our minds to the truth. The sword of the Word is powerful!

The Word of God is so powerful that with the words of Scripture, Jesus drove Satan away from Him in the wilderness. When Jesus fasted for 40 days in the desert in preparation for His ministry, He faced temptations from Satan. How did Jesus respond to Satan and overcome that onslaught of temptation? He quoted Scripture. He demonstrated that the Word of God overcomes temptation. He showed us that the very words of God on the pages of Scripture are filled with power to fight off Satan.

How does quoting Scripture fight off Satan and temptation? It's not simply quoting Scripture, it is having the deep conviction that the Word of God is true and powerful, and we should obey it. When Satan tempted Jesus by telling Him to turn stones into bread, Jesus not only quoted Scripture but obeyed Scripture. He replied by saying,

> *"Man does not live by bread alone." (Matthew 4:4)*

And then He proceeded to continue to fast and resist the temptation to turn stones into bread.

THE WAR CONTINUES

There are two forces at work in this world: good and evil. There is a spiritual battle raging and whether we realize it or not, we are caught up in this struggle. The good news is there is a way to defend ourselves and overcome the evil we are faced with in our lives.

Jesus faced Satan and the temptation that came against Him and overcame the power of evil. Jesus also had the ultimate victory over Satan's most destructive weapon, death. Jesus' resurrection proved that He has power over death. As followers of Jesus, we will also be victorious. We can resist temptation and the evil that comes against us. And we will ultimately overcome death, just as Jesus did, by being raised to eternal life with Him in Heaven.

THE ARMOR OF GOD

The Apostle Paul explains that we need to put on the armor of God in order to stand against the devil and spiritual forces of evil. Below is his description of the armor that we need to equip ourselves with daily:

> "Finally, be strong in the Lord and in his mighty power. Put on the full armor of God, so that you can take your stand against the devil's schemes. For our struggle is not against flesh and blood, but against the rulers, against the authorities, against the powers of this dark world and against the spiritual forces of evil in the heavenly realms. Therefore, put on the full armor of God, so that when the day of evil comes, you may be able to stand your ground, and after you have done everything, to stand. Stand firm then, with the belt of truth buckled around your waist, with the breastplate of righteousness in place, and with your feet fitted with the readiness that comes from the gospel of peace. In addition to all this, take up the shield of faith, with which you can extinguish all the flaming arrows of the evil one. Take the helmet of salvation and the sword of the Spirit, which is the word of God." (Ephesians 6:10-17)

Notice that the sword is the only offensive weapon listed. The other parts of the armor are defensive weapons, including the "belt of truth," the "breastplate of righteousness," the "shield of faith," and the "helmet of salvation." These are indispensable and necessary for battle, but then Paul lists one more weapon: the "sword of the Spirit" which is the Word of God. As an offensive weapon, we need to be proactive, take up the sword, keep it, hold it, and wield it when facing the enemy.

How to Use the Sword

We have such a powerful weapon with the Word of God. It convicts us of sin and divides truth from lies. It strengthens us to stand against evil and drives temptation away from us. But...

Like a real sword, it needs to be used wisely. The Apostle Paul said to Timothy,

> *"Do your best to present yourself to God as one approved, a workman who does not need to be ashamed and who correctly handles the word of truth." (2 Timothy 2:15)*

We don't add to or take away from the Word of God. We don't change it. We understand God's Word in the context in which it was written. If we take a passage out of context, it could change the intent and the meaning altogether. That is why Bible study is so important. Deep study of Scripture helps us to learn about who the particular writer was writing to, what was going on during that time of history, and how we can learn from it and apply it to our lives today.

It is the sword of the Word of God that penetrates and divides truth from error. The truth will anger some people. Jesus said in Matthew 10:34,

> *"Do not suppose that I have come to bring peace to the earth. I did not come to bring peace, but a sword."*

Jesus bringing a "sword"? Isn't Jesus all about peace? Jesus went on to explain that families would be divided because of Him. He wasn't talking about the sword as a military weapon of war. He was saying that the truth divides people and causes disagreements, even among family members.

In a world of war and conflict, doesn't a sword actually bring peace? Think about it. If a sword is not used against evil, then evil wins. Jesus was saying that ultimate peace comes from truth. The sword of the Word of God cuts and exposes the truth. The sword is not like a hammer to be pounded. The sword is a precise weapon that takes skill to wield. And the truth of the Word of God overcomes evil. There is power in the Word of God!

CHAPTER 19

Nourishment for Our Souls

It's surprising how many people nourish and take care of their physical bodies yet ignore the spiritual food they need for their souls. Nourishing our spiritual lives is crucial if we want to be spiritually healthy. What does it mean to be spiritually healthy? It means that we believe and submit to the truth… we repent of any known sin in our lives… we are in a right relationship with God through the Lord Jesus. And we eat daily of God's Word to grow and become a useful servant in the Kingdom of God.

Jeremiah 15:16 says,

> *"When your words came, I ate them; they were my joy and my heart's delight, for I bear your name, O Lord God Almighty."*

Isaiah 55:2 encourages us to eat of God's Word.

> *"Why spend money on what is not bread, and your labor on what does not satisfy? Listen, listen to me, and eat what is good, and your soul will delight in the richest of fare."*

The word "eat" is very descriptive. What it means is that we should read a passage of Scripture and chew on it, meditate on it, think about it, chew again, process it, and chew again. Then we are to swallow it, take it in, let it settle into our minds and hearts. Then we begin to digest it and apply it to our lives. We submit to what it teaches. It becomes part of us.

Jesus plainly said that we should live on God's Word. In other words, we should eat of the Word of God for the sustenance of our very souls.

> "It is written, 'Man does not live on bread alone, but on every word that comes from the mouth of God.'"
> (Matthew 4:4)

When we eat food, we get nourishment and then become hungry again. In the same way, when we eat of God's Word, we are nourished and become hungry for more. In fact, we should keep eating of the Bible, not waiting for a big spiritual hunger pang, in other words, a problem or challenge that makes us starve for God's Word. In order to be spiritually strong and healthy, we should be eating from the pages of Scripture every day.

You've heard the phrase, "you are what you eat." The emphasis is taking care of what we eat, knowing that every bite has an effect on our physical bodies.

What are you eating spiritually? False, feel good, everything's OK philosophies? If you continue consuming empty, feel good philosophies, you will not become spiritually healthy or strong. When you eat of the edifying truth of God's Word, you will find that you are growing stronger on the inside and becoming healthier in your spirit. Just as maintaining physical health must be accomplished by making decisions about exercising, eating healthy foods, and taking vitamins, so it is with our spiritual health. We must be proactive, make the effort to guard our minds and hearts from wrong beliefs, and spend time in God's Word.

How often do you eat? Every day?

Many years ago, I learned that I must take time to eat of God's Word every day. I need that time with the Lord on a daily basis, first thing in the morning, before I face the challenges of everyday life. I learned that morning time with the Lord must be my priority, otherwise the day continues to pile on new things to deal with and think about.

If you own a Bible, or have access to the Bible online, you have healthy spiritual food right there, ready to be eaten and become nourishment for your very soul.

> *"How sweet are your words to my taste, sweeter than honey to my mouth!"*
> *(Psalm 119:103)*

CHAPTER 20

The Depth of the Bible

The Bible is not just a book. It looks like a book; it is bound and has pages and printed words. But if it were just an ordinary book, why do many of us read it every day? We study passages, verses, and books within the Bible. I've been studying the Bible for over 40 years. The more I study, the more there is to learn!

Christians listen to pastors preach entire sermons on verses in the Bible. We read the Bible over and over because there is so much depth that a lifetime of study won't bring us to the point of complete understanding. Why? Because the Bible is the *mind of God*. And God's mind is far beyond what a mere human can comprehend. Each of the 40 authors of the Bible was inspired by the Holy Spirit to write their portion of the message, the story, the history, the lessons, the wisdom, the prophecy, and the deep, deep thoughts of our infinite, all powerful God.

The bestselling book of all time is an extraordinary, fathomless ocean filled with life at all levels. If you explore the depths of the pages of God's powerful Word, you will never reach the bottom of the ocean, the edges of its limits, or the end of its source of life, truth, and wisdom.

If you think it sounds fascinating that there could be a

book with so many amazing attributes, just wait until you dive into its depths and discover treasure that you could never have imagined. You will never reach the limits of the riches of the Word of God!

EASY ENOUGH FOR A CHILD – CHALLENGING ENOUGH FOR BIBLICAL SCHOLARS

God loves every individual person. Some are young, some are middle-aged, some are old. Some are little children and some are intelligent scholars. Some have been taught the Scriptures and some have never owned a Bible. God loves every person; each is a masterpiece of his creation.

It's not surprising that God's message to mankind, His revelation and very words in the Bible, would be simple enough for a youngster to understand, yet profound and challenging enough to keep Biblical scholars searching and learning for centuries.

What is surprising is how God accomplished this great task! How can it be so simple even a child can grasp and believe, yet so complex that scholars analyze single words or phrases for years?

The answer is: the mind of God and the love of God. If you combine the mind of God with the love He has for each and every person, you come to the Bible.

Beginning with the Garden of Eden, how hard is it to understand what it means that Adam and Eve each took a bite out of a piece of fruit? Pretty simple, right? God told them they could eat of any tree in the Garden of Eden, except one. Which tree did they decide to eat from? The only one that was prohibited. Even a child can grasp that concept of disobedience to God.

Yet scholars have studied the Fall of Man for centuries. Why did Adam and Eve make this choice? How did God deal with them afterwards? What happened to creation when God spoke the curses as a result of their sin? What does this mean for mankind? What does this mean for you and me as we navigate life in a fallen world? There is much to pour over and learn from this one event.

Jesus Christ is simple enough for a child to understand and believe. He placed His hands on a blind man and the man could see. Jesus walked on water during a storm that threatened to sink the Disciples' boat. Jesus fed a hungry crowd with just five loaves of bread and two fish. Jesus performs miracles! He also said,

> *"Let the little children come to me, and do not hinder them, for the kingdom of heaven belongs to such as these." (Matthew 19:14)*

Children learn "Jesus loves me" when they are very young. They may not grasp the magnitude of Jesus' sacrifice on the cross or many other deep Biblical principles, but they do know this: Jesus loves me.

Yet the Gospel has more depth than any Bible scholar can possibly dive into and fully comprehend. Bible students, teachers, pastors, and those who love the Scriptures study verse by verse, phrase by phrase, story after story, to glean all of the wonderful truths that are found in each layer of the immense ocean of the Bible.

The Bible is for everyone, young and old, rich and poor, uneducated and scholarly. God's message is for *all* people.

PART 3: THE POWER OF THE BIBLE

THE BIBLE CORRECTS EMPTY RELIGION AND WRONG THEOLOGY

People are created to worship. We long to worship. People everywhere seek religion because it gives them a form, a structure, a way to worship.

Christianity is different from other world religions because it's all about a *relationship* with the living God. Relationship is different from religion. We can practice a form of religion, a form of worship, without having any type of relationship with God Himself.

We can hear sermons and learn about God. We can read books about God. But the Bible contains God's very words. Reading the Bible helps us come to know the heart of God, the character of God, who He is, and how much He loves each of us individually and personally. God revealed His heart, His desires, His love, His anger, and His feelings to the prophets and writers of Scripture.

Hear the heart of God in these words that He spoke to His people through Jeremiah the prophet in Jeremiah chapter 2:

> *"I remember the devotion of your youth, how as a bride you loved me and followed me through the desert...." (vs. 2)*

> *"I brought you into a fertile land to eat its fruit and rich produce. But you came and defiled my land and made my inheritance detestable." (vs. 7)*

> *"I had planted you like a choice vine of sound and reliable stock. How then did you turn against me into a corrupt, wild vine?" (vs. 21)*

> "But you said, 'It's no use! I love foreign gods, and I must go after them.'" (vs. 25)

> "They say to wood, 'You are my father,' and to stone, 'You gave me birth.' They have turned their backs to me and not their faces; yet when they are in trouble, they say, 'Come and save us!'" (vs. 27)

> "Does a young maiden forget her jewelry, a bride her wedding ornaments? Yet my people have forgotten me...." (vs. 32)

Oh, my heart aches when I read those verses! I hear the heart of God who loves His people so much that He compares them to a bride. God reminded them of all He had done for them and they responded by turning their back on Him. They committed spiritual adultery, giving their love and devotion to lifeless, man-made gods. They forgot about God and turned away from Him. Listen to God's heart of grief and His anger when they turn to Him only when they need help. The people knew those wooden, lifeless gods couldn't help them. So, when desperate, they would turn to the true God for help.

I don't know about you, but reading those words, from the mouth of God through the prophet Jeremiah, hits me hard. I even see myself in this passage of love and admonishment. Have I been unfaithful? Following idols of this world? Trusting in lifeless, worthless things and only turning to God when I need help? How that must hurt God!

When we study the Bible, we come to know who God really is. Setting the Bible on a shelf and ignoring His very Word hinders our growth in coming to know God personally. We may depend on a form of religion rather than our relationship with the living God. I have met people who rely on their church attendance, their acts of service, and recitation of certain prayers as their form of worship. Yet they don't have a relationship with the Lord.

Jesus said,

> *"Many will say to me on that day, 'Lord, Lord, did we not prophesy in your name and in your name drive out demons and in your name perform many miracles?' Then I will tell them plainly, 'I never knew you. Away from me, you evildoers!'"*
> (Matthew 7:22-23)

In other words, a person can think he is doing a good thing, accomplishing some good work, even in the name of the Lord. But if there is no personal relationship with Jesus and the person is not indwelt by the Holy Spirit, Jesus will say to him, "I never knew you." It's true, you can have religion without knowing Jesus.

Not only will we rely on a form of religion without the clear teaching of the Bible, but we will also form our own theology. Believe it or not, just about everyone has their own theology or understanding about God. Theology is what we know and believe to be true about God, who He is, how He works, and what His character is like. When you talk with people, you may hear many different theologies or interpretations or understandings about God.

Reading the Bible and learning from it will help us maintain our theology *based on the truth*. The Bible is our plumb line, the truth against which all else is measured. We need to be so familiar with Scripture and know as much as possible that when we hear people state something that is far off from the truth, we can respond with the Truth of God's Word.

Many times, people form their theology from their experiences. They experience suffering, loss of a loved one, loss of a job, or another type of challenge, and conclude that God is not good. God doesn't love them. God doesn't care. So, they explain their suffering by a false theology that is based on their personal experience.

Or people say that God is love; therefore, He loves all people and they are all His children. People can sin, do whatever they want, and no matter what, they will go to Heaven. But the Bible teaches us that God is love and loves everyone, but not all are His children.

The Apostle John tells us,

> *"Yet to all who received him, to those who believed in his name, he gave the right to become children of God – children born not of natural descent, nor of human decision or a husband's will, but born of God." (John 1:12-13)*

Do you see how the Word of God straightens, corrects, and teaches the pure, true theology that we need to understand?

CHAPTER 21

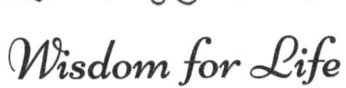

Wisdom for Life

Knowledge. Intellect. Education. Philosophy. Expertise. Learning. Intelligence. Brilliance.

Wisdom is above all those things. Have you ever met people who are very intelligent, learned and scholarly, but lack wisdom? That's because wisdom is in a category of its own. It is above worldly knowledge. It is above what we can learn in school.

Through education we learn facts, data, skills, and various aspects of practical knowledge that help us in life and work. But wisdom is the insight, the discernment, and judgment to be able to use what we learn and rightly apply it.

The third king of Israel, King Solomon, was blessed with great wisdom. When Solomon became king, God said,

> *"Ask for whatever you want me to give you."*
> *(1 Kings 3:5b)*

Solomon answered in humility, not asking for riches or that his enemies would be destroyed, but asking for wisdom:

> *"So give your servant a discerning heart to govern your people and to distinguish between right and wrong. For who is able to govern this great people of yours?" (1 Kings 3:9)*

God was so pleased that Solomon asked for wisdom that He granted him wealth and honor in addition to wisdom. Solomon's desire was to be given wisdom from God so that he could govern the nation of Israel. God responded that He would give Solomon a wise and discerning heart so that

> *"there will never have been anyone like you, nor will there ever be." (1 Kings 3:12b)*

God did exactly what He promised to King Solomon. The Bible explains that God gave Solomon wisdom, great insight, and understanding "as measureless as the sand on the seashore." Solomon's wisdom was greater than all the wisdom of the world, and his fame spread to all the nations. 1 Kings 10:24 says,

> *"The whole world sought audience with Solomon to hear the wisdom God had put in his heart."*

The Queen of Sheba traveled many miles to visit Solomon after hearing about his fame. She wanted to meet Solomon and test him with hard questions. Her story is found in 1 Kings chapter 10 and 2 Chronicles chapter 9. King Solomon answered all of her questions and she was amazed by his wisdom. It is believed that she spent months learning from the wisest person on earth.

We benefit from that marvelous and generous gift of the wisdom of God given to King Solomon. The Bible tells us in 1 Kings 4:32 that Solomon spoke 3,000 proverbs and wrote

1,005 songs! Many of Solomon's proverbs (truth, advice, wisdom) are found right in the Bible.

GOD'S WISDOM

Wisdom can be placed into two categories. Man's wisdom and God's wisdom. People may have a certain measure of worldly wisdom. We might consider a person wise who makes good decisions and has a depth of knowledge and understanding about life. But the wisdom of God is far above human wisdom. It's the mind of God, the truth, and perfect insight.

> *"But the wisdom that comes from heaven is first of all pure; then peace-loving, considerate, submissive, full of mercy and good fruit, impartial and sincere."*
> *(James 3:17)*

If we want to live according to God's will, we should strive for Godly wisdom. It is the wisdom of God that helps us to see things from His perspective and to discern the right responses and actions. Wisdom gives us the ability to judge correctly and act according to the truth. In other words, wisdom is not just knowing the facts but applying the correct judgment and the right action.

I WANT WISDOM!

The words "I want wisdom" become the first step to obtaining it. When we consider how people become wise, the first step is to desire it. I believe that is why God blessed King Solomon with so much wisdom. Solomon desired it!

Do you want wisdom? The book of Proverbs in the Bible is God's wisdom. It is the wisdom that God gave to King

Solomon. We can learn so much by reading the 31 chapters in the book of Proverbs. Solomon explains the origin, value, purpose, and qualities of wisdom. He describes wisdom and contrasts it with foolishness. He describes people who have wisdom. He encourages us to seek, listen, pay attention, and "lay hold of" wisdom. The book of Proverbs is filled with practical, true wisdom.

A proverb is not a rule or a promise. It is a general statement of a principle. It is great advice because the principle is sound, practical truth that helps us in life. Wisdom helps us avoid the pitfalls that are found on the path of sin and foolishness.

Solomon tells us in Proverbs 9:10,

> *"The fear of the Lord is the beginning of wisdom, and knowledge of the Holy One is understanding."*

Solomon was saying that we should have reverence, awe, and respect for God. People who reject God should fear the judgment of God and spending an eternity without Him. On the other hand, the beginning of wisdom is recognizing God for who He is and submitting to Him with awe and respect.

We humble ourselves before our Holy God and admit that we need Him. We worship and obey Him. Without humility we won't obtain wisdom. Without honoring God with awe and respect, true wisdom will be elusive.

One might say, "I'll live my own way, life works just fine when I'm the boss." That may be true to some extent. Human beings can enjoy worldly things and feel the security of money and power. But Proverbs extends warnings to those who trust in themselves and their riches. Solomon warns that our temporal things can be destroyed at any time. We need something else, a rock, a foundation that will keep our feet firm in this tumultuous world. We must seek wisdom, trust in the Lord, and hate wickedness.

> *"When the storm has swept by, the wicked are gone, but the righteous stand firm forever."*
> *(Proverbs 10:25)*

SEEKING WISDOM

The Bible offers so much wisdom that people have no excuse to give in to foolishness. Solomon tells us in Proverbs 4:7,

> *"Wisdom is supreme, therefore get wisdom. Though it cost all you have, get understanding."*

Solomon didn't mean wisdom can be bought. What he meant is that it will cost you. It may mean not spending time with people who are sinning and influencing you in a negative way. It may mean sacrificing your time to study God's Word to gain wisdom. Whatever it might mean for you, there is a cost. Wisdom is not always easily obtained. Temptation must be resisted. Living with integrity can be difficult at times, and patience will be required when pursuing a more righteous life.

Even if people don't have access to the Bible to plainly read proverbs of wisdom, they can learn from other wise people. The book of Proverbs encourages readers to listen to instruction and teaching from people who have already learned (perhaps the hard way) and have gained wisdom and understanding from life experiences. Proverbs 1:8 says,

> *"Listen, my son, to your father's instruction and do not forsake your mother's teaching."*

We are not to object to discipline, as it leads to correction and understanding.

Solomon tells us that wisdom calls to us, even from out in the street.

> *"Wisdom calls aloud in the street, she raises her voice in the public squares; at the head of the noisy streets she cries out, in the gateways of the city she makes her speech." (Proverbs 1:20-21)*

When we witness foolishness in the streets and hear about sin in the news, the wise person will be convicted of what is right and wrong. Wisdom is actually crying out for people to shun evil and seek out what is true and right. Solomon goes on to explain in verses 24-25 that people ignore wisdom's advice and do not accept wisdom's rebuke. Those who reject wisdom will "eat the fruit of their ways." (Proverbs 1:31)

Seeking wisdom means seeking God, because wisdom comes from the mind of God. We seek wisdom in the pages of Proverbs and the rest of the Scriptures. We seek by listening to faithful pastors and Bible teachers who explain the Word of God. We seek by resisting the evil around us. We seek wisdom no matter what the cost.

OBTAINING WISDOM

When we seek wisdom, how does wisdom come to us? Do we wake up a little wiser? Do we suddenly find we have the right answers to our problems? Do we begin to give better advice to others?

The book of James gives us a very simple instruction to obtain wisdom. James 1:5 tells us that we should pray for God to give us more wisdom. James tells us that this is a prayer that God is very generous in answering!

> *"If any of you lacks wisdom, he should ask God, who gives generously to all without finding fault, and it will be given to him." (James 1:5)*

The request for the precious gift of wisdom is answered with a warning. James goes on to say in verses 6-8,

> *"But when he asks, he must believe and not doubt, because he who doubts is like a wave of the sea, blown and tossed by the wind. That man should not think he will receive anything from the Lord. He is a double-minded man, unstable in all he does."*

We need to ask in faith and not doubt. God will give us wisdom. We are to commit to living by the wisdom God gives, not wavering between what is right and the temptations of the world. Wisdom demands commitment, faithfulness, and stability; foolishness comes from continuing to desire the sinful ways of the world. Vacillating between two worlds makes us "double-minded," "tossed by the wind," and "unstable."

The prayer for wisdom opens our minds and hearts to the wisdom we learn from Scripture, Godly pastors, and the Holy Spirit directly speaking to our hearts. Becoming wiser is a daily process as we seek the Lord every day through prayer and study of God's Word.

OBEYING WISDOM

This is the hard part! In fact, disobedience to what we know is wise and true is the single most important factor to the downfall of "wise" people. It is the obedience to wisdom and following the voice of wisdom that truly makes a person wise.

PART 3: THE POWER OF THE BIBLE

If you are familiar with King Solomon's life, you know that even though he was the wisest person who ever lived, there came a time when he messed up so badly that the entire kingdom was split into two nations, no longer united as one. How could this happen to the greatest and wisest king this world has ever known?

2 Chronicles 7:11-22 explains the blessings the Lord promised Solomon if he obeyed God's commands and walked with Him faithfully, as his father David did. But the passage also describes the consequences if Solomon turned away and served other gods. This is exactly what Solomon eventually did. He had 700 wives and 300 concubines. He married the daughters of foreign rulers. These wives brought their pagan gods and Solomon allowed them to continue to worship what they knew. Soon their presence influenced King Solomon and he became half-hearted toward the Lord. 1 Kings 11:4 tells us,

> *"As Solomon grew old, his wives turned his heart after other gods, and his heart was not fully devoted to the Lord his God, as the heart of David his father had been."*

We learn more about Solomon's sin in 1 Kings 11:9-10.

> *"The Lord became angry with Solomon because his heart had turned away from the Lord, the God of Israel, who had appeared to him twice. Although he had forbidden Solomon to follow other gods, Solomon did not keep the Lord's command."*

The passage goes on to say in verse 11 that God would "tear" the kingdom away from Solomon.

You might ask, *Why would God be so angry just because*

people worship other gods? God's commands are not just whims from a God who wants to be worshipped. No, when sinful human beings worship other gods, just imagine how their practices become evil, sinful, and detestable to the Lord. The blessings that the Lord wants to provide become skewed, marred, and destroyed. 1 Kings 11:7 explains,

> *"On a hill east of Jerusalem, Solomon built a high place for Chemosh the detestable god of Moab, and for Molech the detestable god of the Ammonites. He did the same for all his foreign wives, who burned incense and offered sacrifices to their gods."*

Big deal? To each his own method of worship? No, God expects full allegiance, loyalty, faithfulness, and no less. The pagan religions weren't methods of worship that could mix with Judaism. The Bible records that ancient people sacrificed their own children's lives to the pagan god of Moab (Chemosh) and the pagan god of the Ammonites (Molech). (2 Kings 3:27, Jeremiah 32:35, 1 Kings 11:7) Pagan worship produces death, pain, and fruitlessness. It's no wonder that God was so angry with Solomon!

Wisdom is a precious gift of the mind of God to those who seek Him. But wisdom's partner is obedience. If we don't obey wisdom, then how can wisdom serve us? Wisdom isn't what is "best" in our eyes according to our own common sense. Wisdom is the will of God, the mind of God, and His thoughts about every aspect of life.

King Solomon had many successes, and he has gone down in history as the greatest king the world has ever known. But he failed to obey the voice of wisdom when choosing his wives. He made decisions based on the world's standards. In ancient times it was acceptable for kings to marry many women. So that's what King Solomon did. He followed the world's customs and disobeyed God's commands. Failing at one point or making one mistake can change our entire lives. King Solomon was strong and wise but failed to consistently obey all the wisdom he had been given.

If desire and seeking are the keys to obtaining wisdom, obedience is the lock that secures our minds, hearts, and lives. Obedience is the protection, the safety, the wall around us.

SHARING WISDOM

People love to share their experiences with others. They love to tell stories of where they've been, what they've done, and what they know. Many people also love to help others. In my recruiting career, I interviewed many job seekers who relayed to me that they wanted to help others. I have met a lot of "helpers" in my life. If you have a problem, they will share what they have learned from their experiences.

Studying God's Word helps the "helpers" know how to help. Wisdom equips Christians with the ability to share God's mind with others. There are many self-help books available, all with advice to apply to life's problems. But wisdom is advice from God's perspective. Don't we all want to know what God might have to say about our problems and circumstances? When someone comes to you for help, the person's deeper cry may be, "Please, give me something I can hold on to! I need truth, I need hope!"

Not only should we seek and obey wisdom, but we study the Bible in order to share the precious gift of wisdom with others.

CHAPTER 22

The Power to Save

The Bible is the powerful Word of God that is able to penetrate our hearts and convict us of sin. It teaches us the message of the Gospel that brings salvation to those who believe. Romans 1:16 says,

> "I am not ashamed of the gospel because it is the power of God for the salvation of everyone who believes: first for the Jew, then for the Gentile."

Some people might wonder what they need to be "saved" from. All people are sinners and are born separated from God. Romans 3:23 says,

> "For all have sinned and fall short of the glory of God."

We are separated from God by sin and the consequence of sin is death. Romans 6:23 tells us,

> "For the wages of sin is death, but the gift of God is eternal life in Christ Jesus our Lord."

Therefore, we need to be saved from death, eternal misery, and separation from God for all eternity. We must become reconciled to God and receive the eternal life that He offers to us.

Everyone who is alive on this earth today is one day closer to the day they will leave this earth. We will all live for eternity, either with the Lord or, if we have rejected His offer of reconciliation, separated forever from the Lord.

Some believe that our eternal destiny is determined and that God has already decided where each person will spend eternity. They believe that God has made the decision for you. But the Bible clearly teaches that mankind has been given free will. We are free to respond, repent, and accept the gift of salvation, or rebel and refuse Jesus' offer of forgiveness. The reason people are not saved is due to their unbelief, refusal to repent of their sin, and rebellion against God. Plain and simple.

> *"They perish because they refused to love the truth and so be saved." (2 Thessalonians 2:10b)*

Who does God choose for eternal life in Heaven? He chooses those who *place their faith in Jesus*. The glorious invitation to be saved is summed up in John 3:16:

> *"For God so loved the world that he gave his one and only Son, that whoever believes in him shall not perish but have eternal life."*

Whoever believes will be forgiven and receive eternal life. The invitation is for everyone!

> *"Everyone who calls on the name of the Lord will be saved." (Romans 10:13)*

The Bible tells us in 2 Timothy 3:15 that the Scriptures are able to make us "wise for salvation through faith in Christ Jesus." The words on the pages of the Bible will convict us of sin. Those who *repent* and *believe* in the Lord Jesus will be saved. In that moment! The Holy Spirit takes the Word of God and accomplishes the powerful work of salvation in the hearts of those who believe. When you hear God's Word, repent of your sin, and place your faith in Jesus Christ, you will be saved. That's the promise of the Gospel message.

Do you feel different when you become saved? Many times the answer is a resounding "Yes!" The change is obvious and your life has been redirected completely. Or you may not realize that you've changed until time passes and you begin to see things differently. Your mind is on the Lord, your heart reacts in a new way to the challenges you face, you've lost your appetite for the sin you've been indulging in, and you have new hope for your life. Oh yes, there's a change in you! And deep inside you know you'll never go back. You are on a new path.

Jesus explained this in John chapter 3. He stated in verse 3,

> *"I tell you the truth, no one can see the kingdom of God unless he is born again."*

Since we are born spiritually dead, we must be born anew to be alive spiritually. In verses 5-6, Jesus said,

> *"I tell you the truth, no one can enter the kingdom of God unless he is born of water and the Spirit. Flesh gives birth to flesh, but the Spirit gives birth to spirit."*

Becoming "born again" means our spirit has been given new life. We are made alive spiritually. And Jesus points out that no one will enter the kingdom of God unless they are made alive by the power of the Holy Spirit.

Jesus used the term "born again" when describing salvation. When a baby is born, the baby can never go back into the mother's womb. The birth is permanent, the baby has passed from the old life to a new life. This term gives us confidence when wondering if we can lose the salvation that we were granted upon believing in Jesus. He made it clear that if we are made alive spiritually, we are born anew, there's no going back! We may fail, we may sin, we may be disobedient. But as a child who is born to parents, he is loved no matter what, and there is no way to "undo" the birth.

At the moment of salvation, a Believer is born anew and sealed by the Holy Spirit with a seal that can never be broken. Ephesians 1:13 explains salvation with these words,

> *"And you also were included in Christ when you heard the word of truth, the gospel of your salvation. Having believed, you were marked in him with a seal, the promised Holy Spirit."*

In John 14:16 Jesus promised to send Believers the Holy Spirit to live inside of us permanently, and give us life, counsel, comfort, and strength. This happens when we believe; when we turn to the Lord with a repentant heart and place our faith in Him. This is an intimate moment between you and your Savior. It is the moment when you finally choose to turn from your sin and receive the forgiveness and reconciliation with God that Jesus accomplished on the cross.

Jesus said in John 6:63,

> *"The Spirit gives life; the flesh counts for nothing. The words I have spoken to you are spirit and they are life."*

SANCTIFICATION

Not only is there life in the Word of God, but there is tremendous power to make us more like Christ. The Word of God *produces* righteousness. Salvation happens in a moment and righteousness grows. Growth and maturity take time. Isaiah 45:8 tells us that salvation "springs up" and righteousness grows with it. This is an extremely important verse as it reveals the truth about salvation; it is instant and irreversible. However, our sanctification is a process; it is not instantaneous. The righteousness that we desire grows. And growing is a process. Little by little. Step by step. From glory to glory. (2 Corinthians 3:18)

Imagine a plant that springs out of the ground, breaking the soil, and emerging with life. Then the plant or flower continues to grow, slowly but surely, steadily and faithfully, growing up into a full-grown plant or bloom of a flower. We grow every day by continuing to read the Bible, eating of God's Word, praying for wisdom, and living in obedience to what we learn. Sanctification is the growth that Believers go through in their lives as Christians. This is the process of being purified from sin and becoming more like Christ.

Ephesians 5:26 refers to the Bible as the "water" of the Word. Water cleanses and takes away impurities. We wash things with water that carries the dirt away. After we receive salvation by the power of God's Word, we become sanctified by that same power.

> *"Sanctify them by the truth; your word is truth."*
> *(John 17:17)*

The Holy Spirit takes the Word of God and sanctifies us by convicting us of sin, changing our desires, and helping us to live in obedience. As we continue reading the Word of God and listening to Biblical preaching, we go through the process of becoming more like Christ.

This is what God wants to accomplish in the lives of Believers. The Bible says plainly in 1 Thessalonians 4:3a,

> *"It is God's will that you should be sanctified...."*

We should not become discouraged, nor should we stifle our sanctification and spiritual growth by continuing to live a lifestyle of sin. The Holy Spirit will complete this work within us. Philippians 1:6 promises,

> *"...being confident of this, that he who began a good work in you will carry it on to completion until the day of Christ Jesus."*

TODAY'S THE DAY

I'm not ready yet. Someday I'll consider this. When the time is right, I'll go to church. I'll deal with this later. Later... Later... Later.

If you have found yourself saying any of those statements, the Bible firmly responds by saying,

> *"I tell you, now is the time of God's favor, now is the day of salvation." (2 Corinthians 6:2b)*

Why is it so important to believe today? What is wrong with putting off our response to a more convenient time?

If you are not willing to believe today, you could become unable to believe tomorrow. Though God can and will save whoever turns to Him in repentance and faith, the Bible warns against hardening our hearts and continuing in rebellion. Psalm 95:7b-8a says,

> "Today, if you hear his voice, do not harden your hearts."

The Gospel message pierces and softens the hearts of those who hear it. If they intentionally persist in unbelief, their hearts become hardened. Exodus 7:14 tells us that Pharoah's heart was unyielding. He refused many times to obey God's command to release the Israelites from slavery. After many appeals, God finally had enough of Pharoah's rebellion, and Exodus 10:1 says that God hardened Pharoah's heart. This was the judgment of God on an already hardened, rebellious heart.

On the other hand, if those who hear the Gospel message respond to the truth, God will strengthen them in their willingness to turn from their sin and begin their walk of faith with the Lord. He will continue to soften a heart that is submissive to Him.

Another reason that responding today is so important is: God's invitation for salvation is for those alive on earth. Judgment comes after our life ends and we face the Lord. Do you know how long you will live? No one knows if they will have tomorrow.

Today is the best day to believe and accept the invitation of salvation and God's grace in your life!

EXPERIENCING THE POWER OF THE BIBLE

As you study Scripture, your faith will grow. Faith is a gift from God that He gives to those who seek Him. Ephesians 2:8-9 explains:

PART 3: THE POWER OF THE BIBLE

> *"For it is by grace you have been saved, through faith—and this is not from yourselves, it is the gift of God—not by works, so that no one can boast."*

What is faith?

> *"Now faith is being sure of what we hope for and certain of what we do not see." (Hebrews 11:1)*

Faith means trusting God. Do you want more faith?

Our faith increases as we read or hear God's Word. Romans 10:17 explains:

> *"Consequently, faith comes from hearing the message, and the message is heard through the word of Christ."*

The gift of faith is given through the Word of God.

Keep reading the Bible. Obey what you believe God has shown you to do. Keep reading. Seek the Lord with all your heart. Keep reading. Pray for the Holy Spirit to help you understand God's Word. The Bible has the power to save you and transform you and your faith will grow.

CHAPTER 23

The Power of God's Will Revealed

What is God's will... What is His will for mankind... What is God's will for me?

The answers to those important questions are found in the Bible. Many people wonder what God's will is and pray to Him to find out. They may seek His will by asking friends or their pastor. It is a challenge to know and understand what God's plan is for us and what He wants us to do.

Why is God's will so (seemingly) elusive? If God really loves the masterpiece of His creation and wants to be in a relationship with us, why is it so hard to figure out what He wants from us?

God's will is not as elusive as some may believe. Much of His will is clearly written in the Bible. If it seems that God's will is hard to find in the Bible, we must continue to search for it on the pages of Scripture. I have learned over the years that if something is hard to find in the Bible, it could be because God wants us to dig for it. This is a great principle of Scripture. Will we dig deeper? Will we continue to study the Bible and search for His will? Our response to the challenge of finding God's will reveals what is really in our hearts.

Am I seeking a deeper relationship with Him or simply seeking His blessing in my life?

Am I searching for God's stamp of approval on my desires and my plan?

Am I submissive and ready to obey God's will when I learn what He wants from me?

Will I give up when I disagree or don't like what God speaks to me through His Word?

Am I willing to repent and turn from my sin as the Holy Spirit convicts my heart?

Is Jesus really Lord of my life?

THE HOLY SPIRIT REVEALS...

The Bible tells us that it is the Spirit of God that teaches us and helps us to understand the "deep things of God." 1 Corinthians 2:10-12 says,

> *"...but God has revealed it to us by His Spirit. The Spirit searches all things, even the deep things of God. For who among men knows the thoughts of a man except the man's spirit within him? In the same way no one knows the thoughts of God except the Spirit of God. We have not received the spirit of the world, but the Spirit who is from God, so that we may understand what God has freely given us."*

It is a powerful and wonderful thing to have the Holy Spirit living within us. God Himself, residing within us to seal us, guide us, comfort us, counsel us, and reveal to us the deep truths of the revelation of God on the pages of Scripture.

God is always ready to be closer and understandable to those who seek Him. God spoke through the prophet Jeremiah,

> *"This is what the Lord says, he who made the earth, the Lord who formed it and established it – the Lord is his name: 'Call to me and I will answer you and tell you great and unsearchable things you do not know.'" (Jeremiah 33:2-3)*

I love that verse! I have personally experienced the Holy Spirit revealing deeper things in Scripture as I called out to God in prayer. But notice what Jeremiah reminds the reader in verse 2, right before quoting the words of God. He reminds us that God created and established all things and He is Lord. In other words, we need to recognize and worship God for who He truly is before calling on His name.

MORE LIGHT IS GIVEN WHEN YOU OBEY

I have good news and bad news for you. The bad news first. If you don't obey the little that you do understand, God will not give deeper understanding of greater things. He won't shine more light onto the pages of Scripture if you refuse to obey the light that has already been given to you.

The good news is the opposite. If you obey the little that you do know and understand from Scripture, the Holy Spirit will give you more light to understand the deeper things of God. We live by faith and walk little by little, step by step through our journey of faith with the Lord. We are to strive, search, and seek God's will diligently in the Bible. When we seek the Lord, our relationship with Him deepens and strengthens, as any relationship would when you spend time with someone. As our relationship with God grows, we are faced with learning more about ourselves, what needs to change, and what God is calling us to do. We allow ourselves to be convicted by what we read. We are willing to go through the discomfort of repenting, changing, and choosing to walk according to God's will.

When we don't understand or feel our prayers are not being answered, we delve deeper into the pages of Scripture, seeking, pleading, praying, searching. If you've been there, you know that during those times of seeking the Lord, He changes us, refines us, convicts us, and helps us to see things more clearly from His perspective. We are human beings seeking the mind of the Almighty God. And God has made a way for us to learn, grow, and understand. But we must be faithful and obedient to things that we already know.

In fact, James 1:25 tells us that we are to persist and continue looking into the Word of God.

> *"But the man who looks intently into the perfect law that gives freedom, and continues to do this—not forgetting what he has heard, but doing it—he will be blessed in what he does."*

The word "intently" means to be purposeful and determined. We are not to read God's Word and then promptly go out and continue to live in sin. We are not to be lazy about what we are learning, rather "intently" study the Bible, changing our mind and making a decision to obey what we learn.

GOD'S REVEALED WILL FOR ALL PEOPLE

God's will for the people He created can be found in the pages of Scripture. In the passages below, you'll read specifics about God's will for all people:

✦ *It is God's will for us to repent of our sin.*

> "The Lord is not slow in keeping his promise, as some understand slowness. He is patient with you, not wanting anyone to perish, but everyone to come to repentance." (2 Peter 3:9)

- ✝ It is God's will that people be saved and know the truth.

> "...who wants all men to be saved and come to a knowledge of the truth." (1 Timothy 2:4)

- ✝ It is God's will for us to love others.

> "My command is this: Love each other as I have loved you." (John 15:12)

- ✝ It is God's will that we turn to Jesus for rest.

> "Come to me, all you who are weary and burdened, and I will give you rest." (Matthew 11:28)

- ✝ It is God's will for us to pray in all circumstances.

> "Be joyful always, pray continually, give thanks in all circumstances, for this is God's will for you in Christ Jesus." (1 Thessalonians 5:16)

- ✝ It is God's will for us to be pure.

> "It is God's will that you should be sanctified: that you should avoid sexual immorality...." (1 Thessalonians 4:3)

- ✝ It is God's will that we seek wisdom.

> "If any of you lacks wisdom, you should ask God, who gives generously to all without finding fault, and it will be given to you." (James 1:5)

PART 3: THE POWER OF THE BIBLE

+ *It is God's will that we trust in Him and not rely on our own understanding of things.*

> "Trust in the Lord with all your heart and lean not on your own understanding; in all your ways acknowledge him, and he will make your paths straight." (Proverbs 3:5-6)

+ *It is God's will that we seek His will. We should pray for His will to be done.*

> "...your kingdom come, your will be done, on earth as it is in heaven." (Matthew 6:10)

+ *It is God's will that we do not get drunk, but instead to be filled with the Holy Spirit.*

> "Be very careful, then, how you live—not as unwise but as wise, making the most of every opportunity, because the days are evil. Therefore do not be foolish, but understand what the Lord's will is. Do not get drunk on wine, which leads to debauchery. Instead, be filled with the Spirit." (Ephesians 5:15-18)

+ *It is God's will that we confess our sins.*

> "If we confess our sins, he is faithful and just and will forgive us our sins and purify us from all unrighteousness." (1 John 1:9)

+ *It is God's will for us to be humble, merciful, and act justly toward others.*

> "He has shown you, O man, what is good. And what does the Lord require of you? To act justly and to love mercy and to walk humbly with your God." (Micah 6:8)

✝ *It is God's will that we persevere.*

> "You need to persevere so that when you have done the will of God, you will receive what he has promised." (Hebrews 10:36)

BUT WHAT ABOUT GOD'S SPECIFIC PLAN FOR MY LIFE?

God has a plan for each of us, something He wants us to accomplish for His Kingdom, whether it is helping your own family, being a witness in your workplace, serving in a ministry, or following the Lord in something else that He is calling you to do.

In order to learn and know God's personal and specific will for our lives, we have to understand how God leads us individually.

We cover all things in prayer. The Apostle Paul tells us to pray "unceasingly." (1 Thessalonians 5:17) Prayer is our direct communication to God. Our intimate relationship with God is strengthened when we rely on Him in prayer. If we want to know God's mind on the matters that concern us, the first thing we must do is pray. We ask God to show us His will and which way we should go.

> "Show me the way I should go, for to you I lift up my soul." (Psalm 143:8b)

Many of David's Psalms are prayers. We can use the words of verses in the Bible in our own prayers.

PART 3: THE POWER OF THE BIBLE

> *"Teach me to do your will, for you are my God."*
> *(Psalm 143: 10a)*

When we pray about a situation, we watch for His hand at work. It is amazing to experience God's answers to our specific prayers!

The Spirit leads us. He does this in many ways. He may impress something on our hearts. He may speak to us through another person. The Holy Spirit may reveal something to us in our minds, granting us wisdom concerning a decision. The Holy Spirit indwells the Christian and works powerfully to counsel, guide, convict, teach, comfort, and lead us. The Holy Spirit guides us into all truth. (John 16:13) We must trust the invisible Holy Spirit. Our part is to seek Him and submit to Him every day.

Listen to His voice. As sheep know the voice of their shepherd, we recognize the voice of our Shepherd. (John 10:3) When we spend time in God's Word, we become more attuned to His voice which speaks to us from the pages of Scripture. The world's system is constantly sending messages to us, even shouting what it wants us to know, but we must learn how to listen to the whisper of God's voice. Psalm 46:10a says,

> *"Be still and know that I am God."*

Being still is difficult. We want to be busy working and doing life. But if we don't quiet our hearts before the Lord, we may miss His voice.

Test God's will. When we sift through all of the influences and information that come at us as we make decisions, the Bible tells us to test and approve what God's will is for us. In other words, we should be able to test what we hear and discern whether it is from the Lord. We pray about opportunities and the counsel we receive from others. We measure these against the Word of God. If it goes against what the Bible teaches, then it is not God's will.

Seeking God's will means trusting Him completely. What we are doing today may be a stepping stone to another point in the journey of God's plan. He may bring opportunities into our lives and direct us specifically to certain tasks. At times, we may be in training or being prepared for something to come in the future.

There is nothing more fulfilling than seeking and discovering God's plan for your life!

CHAPTER 24

Power to Live the Christian Life

The Christian life can be exciting, don't you agree? When I read the Bible, the history, and the stories of how God helped His people, I am amazed. There are no books or movies that compare with the reality of God interacting in miraculous ways with His people.

Even in my own life, I have experienced answers to prayers and God's guidance in ways that have left me awestruck and humbled. I wouldn't want to live any other way than in an intimate, close walk with the Lord.

Some people only call on the Lord when they are in trouble, in the midst of a crisis, or need a miracle. When God works in a marvelous way and the crisis is resolved, they revert back to running their own lives, placing the Bible back on a shelf.

In between the valley and the mountaintop experiences, what does our faith really look like?

During the normal daily routine of life is when people may slowly begin to weaken spiritually. The frustrations, aggravations, and challenges of daily life can quickly bring us down. The world around us constantly presses in on us with temptations to place worldly things above our relationship with the Lord. Soon another crisis comes and we cry out to the Lord for help.

That was the pattern of the ancient Hebrew people. As they mixed with pagan people, they were drawn away from the pure worship of Jehovah God. They began to worship other gods and mix their worship of God with pagan idol worship. Though they were living in covenant with God, they failed in their side of the covenant relationship over and over again. When things got really bad and their enemies began to take them over, they would repent and cry out to God for help.

God would miraculously help; He would raise up a judge or a king to lead and save them from their enemies. God would demonstrate His faithfulness to Israel. His people would experience peace for a while and then the cycle of sin, suffering, repentance, and restoration would begin all over again.

As we read the Old Testament, we see ourselves in this pattern. That's why we study the lives of God's people in the Old Testament. We learn that many people believed on the mountaintop but doubted God and complained in the valley. We learn from those who sinned greatly during moments of unbelief. We also become inspired by those who persevered in their faith in the dungeon as well as the palace. We witness the faithfulness of those who never doubted God. We are convicted by some and inspired by others. We see a little bit of ourselves in all of them.

Isn't the Christian life supposed to be much smoother than that? Why all of the ups and downs?

It took me a long time to learn a very important truth. *Christians are not able to live the Christian life on their own.* Jesus never expected us to be able to follow Him and live the Christian life with our own strength. The Disciples physically walked with Jesus day after day, learning from Him and watching Him miraculously feed 5,000 people, calm the storm, and heal the sick. Jesus prayed with them, taught them, and lived with them. Then, in preparation for leaving them permanently, Jesus said in John 14:16,

> *"And I will ask the Father, and he will give you another Counselor to be with you forever—the Spirit of truth."*

In the original Greek language, this statement carries a deeper meaning than we express in English. Jesus was telling His Disciples that He would send another "Me," someone identical to Me, someone just like Me. That is very powerful, isn't it? The Holy Spirit isn't just a spiritual counselor or helper, He is God Himself, living within us. The Holy Spirit, who is just like Jesus, comes to live within the Believer.

> *"When the Counselor comes, whom I will send to you from the Father, the Spirit of truth who goes out from the Father, he will testify about me."*
> *(John 15:26)*

In fact, when Jesus appeared to the Disciples after His resurrection, He told them in Luke 24:49 to stay in the city until they were "clothed with power from on high." He didn't want them to go out to begin their ministries in their own strength. He instructed them to wait until they were filled with the power of the Holy Spirit.

God never expected us to live as followers of Jesus all on our own. We are saved by His power and grace and we live the Christian life by that same power and grace. We didn't get saved one day by His power and then left to struggle through life using our own strength. The Apostle Paul admonishes those who believe that they are to live the Christian life in their own power.

> *"Are you so foolish? After beginning with the Spirit, are you now trying to attain your goal by human effort?" (Galatians 3:3)*

We as Believers have the Holy Spirit permanently inside of us, so we don't have to live even one day without the strength and help of God Himself.

Why do we need so much help? There are several reasons.

First of all, followers of Jesus are a minority in a culture that believes and thinks totally differently. We are ambassadors in a world not our own. Yet the world's system is all around us, tempting us to stray from God and lose our strength, rendering us useless as servants of the Lord.

Secondly, there is an enemy who has been around since the beginning of time. He tempted Adam and Eve, causing devastating consequences that we are still experiencing today. Satan attacks Believers and wants to destroy our witness for Christ and debilitate us so that we can't accomplish the purpose God has for us.

Thirdly, our own flesh is weak, including our mind, our will, and our emotions. Even as Christians with a new nature, we are still prone to sin and need to rely on the Holy Spirit to strengthen us to follow Jesus. We can be our own worst enemy by not resisting sin and allowing our thoughts to drag us down. Low self-esteem, inadequacies, and discouragement are enemies from within us that keep us from being victorious Christians.

In other words, we have three major enemies: Satan, the world, and ourselves.

What can the Bible do to help us live our daily lives as Spirit-filled Christians? How does the Holy Spirit empower us to live out what we believe?

EVERY DAY... ONE DAY AT A TIME... STEP BY STEP

You may know the story of the manna in the desert. The Israelites had just been freed from 400 years of slavery in Egypt. They were out in the desert and hungry. God miraculously provided bread, literally from Heaven, called "manna." His instructions were to go out in the morning and collect what they needed for one day. The only exception to that was the day before the Sabbath. They were then allowed to collect enough for two days. The purpose was to teach them that they had to have fresh faith every morning. They weren't being asked to rely on yesterday's miracles or yesterday's faith. God did not want them believing that faith today could be stored up for tomorrow. Each morning they were to trust God for that day. God would provide for and sustain them.

Fast forward to the New Testament when Jesus spoke to a crowd of listeners. In John 6:32-35 Jesus tells them that it wasn't Moses who provided the bread in the desert, it is God who gives "true bread from Heaven." Verse 33 says,

> *"For the bread of God is he who comes down from heaven and gives life to the world."*

Then Jesus declared,

> *"I am the bread of life." (verse 35)*

Friends, we are to "eat" of the Bread of Life every day, one day at a time, and step by step in our life's journey. We study Scripture every day, pray continually, and follow the guidance of the Holy Spirit in all things.

The power of the Holy Spirit blesses us in the following ways:

We will know which way to turn. Isaiah 30:21 says,

> *"Whether you turn to the right or to the left, your ears will hear a voice behind you, saying, 'This is the way; walk in it.'"*

Although we don't hear an audible voice, we will recall a Bible verse or hear the voice of our conscience concerning the matter. We will know in our heart what the leading of the Holy Spirit is in the matter of concern.

God speaks to us by the power of the Holy Spirit. Reading, studying, and meditating on the Word of God enables us to receive the truth. We begin to understand things from God's perspective. Each day the Holy Spirit sheds light on our life's path so that we don't stumble and fall. Psalm 119:105 proclaims,

> *"Your word is a lamp to my feet and a light for my path."*

The Holy Spirit living inside of us is the closest, most intimate relationship that we will ever know!

PART 4

The Star of the Bible

CHAPTER 25

Who is the Star of the Bible?

You guessed it, the Star of the Bible is Jesus! He is not only the Star of the New Testament but also the Hero and Star of the entire Bible. As you grow in your Christian journey, you will come to understand that Jesus is undeniably present in the Old Testament and the focus of the New Testament.

In fact, a one sentence overview of Jesus as the Star of the Bible is this:

The Old Testament reveals that the Messiah is coming, the Gospels tell of Jesus, the Messiah who came, and Revelation prophesies that Jesus is coming again.

How could a compilation of 66 books written over the course of 1,500 years by over 40 different authors somehow point to one person whose ministry lasted a mere 3 years?

The answer is this: The God of the Universe was sovereignly in control of the inspiration, the writing, and the compilation of the book that we call *The Bible*.

The first hint of Jesus comes as a prophecy stated in Genesis chapter 3. God's creation was perfect, including the two people He created, Adam and Eve. Satan, God's enemy, wanted to destroy what God had created and tempted Adam and Eve to disobey God's command not to eat from the tree of knowledge of good and evil. Adam and Eve disobeyed and ate fruit of the tree, breaking their fellowship with God and introducing sin, rebellion, and suffering into the world.

Where did the enemy of God come from? Satan was an angel who became filled with pride and wanted to be equal to God. Therefore, God cast him out of Heaven. You may learn more about this former angel who became the devil in Isaiah 14:12, Ezekiel 28:17, and Revelation 12:9.

God placed a curse on Satan stating,

> *"And I will put enmity between you and the woman, and between your offspring and hers; he will crush your head and you will strike his heel."*
> *(Genesis 3:15)*

This is the first evidence of the Gospel to come much later. God explained that someone would come and deliver a crushing, fatal blow to Satan and that Satan would inflict a bruise, a non-fatal blow to the heel of that person.

When Adam and Eve sinned against God, they introduced sin into the world. The consequence resulted in a curse on them and the physical world. Later, someone would come and undo the curse, taking away the sin of the world.

Who is this one who was to come? Who is the one prophesied about in Genesis 3:15?

The Bible answers that question in the pages of Scripture. From Genesis to Revelation, the identity of this person is revealed as Jesus, the Messiah, the Christ, the Savior.

JESUS IN THE OLD TESTAMENT

Every book of the Old Testament provides a picture, an example, a description, a shadow of the Savior to come. As we study the Old Testament, we learn aspects of the character of Jesus, His titles, His roles, what He does for His people, and the depth of His personality. The range of expressions about Jesus in the Old Testament books is amazing. Here are some examples:

- ✛ Exodus: Jesus is our Passover Lamb
- ✛ Leviticus: He is our High Priest
- ✛ Ruth: He is our Redeemer
- ✛ Esther: He is the Sovereign God
- ✛ Proverbs: He is our Wisdom
- ✛ Isaiah: Jesus is the Wonderful Counselor, Mighty God, Everlasting Father, and Prince of Peace
- ✛ Hosea: He is faithful to the unfaithful

Every book of the Old Testament provides a correlation to our Savior who is presented in the New Testament. The books of the Old Testament prepared God's people to recognize Jesus as the fulfillment of all that the Old Testament Scriptures illuminated about the coming Messiah.

After His resurrection, Jesus appeared to two Disciples on the road to Emmaus. Jesus explained how He fulfilled what the Scriptures foretold about Him. Luke 24:25-27 says:

> "He said to them, 'How foolish you are, and how slow of heart to believe all that the prophets have spoken! Did not the Christ have to suffer these things and then enter his glory?' And beginning with Moses and all the Prophets, he explained to them what was said in all the Scriptures concerning himself."

We have the same Old Testament books that Jesus explained to the Disciples that day. Jesus proved to them through the Scriptures that He is the foretold Messiah. As we study the Old Testament, we already know the answer to the question, *Who is this Savior to come?*

JESUS IN THE NEW TESTAMENT

The four Gospels that begin the New Testament tell us about Jesus' birth, ministry, death, and resurrection.

The New Testament epistles continue to describe and explain our mighty Savior as well as address specific churches on matters of doctrine. The book of Revelation is the final chapter of this world and the victory of Jesus over sin, Satan, and evil forever.

Below is a snapshot of Jesus portrayed in the New Testament:

- Matthew: Jesus is King
- Mark: Jesus is servant
- Luke: Jesus is the Savior
- John: Jesus is the Son of God
- 1 & 2 Timothy: Jesus is our mediator
- Hebrews: Jesus is our great High Priest
- Revelation: Jesus is the King of Kings!

When we read through the books of the Bible, we are seeing glimpses of individual threads that are woven together into a larger story. We look closely at each thread portrayed throughout the Scriptures. Moving on through the books we discover more unique threads, each adding its own aspect to the essence of the greater message. When we have read through the entire Bible, we step back and look at the whole story and marvel, *Now I understand how all the threads are woven together to make one beautiful tapestry!*

CHAPTER 26

The Shadow of Jesus

A few years ago, I began to have a greater understanding of the importance of a shadow. I had never given it much thought. After all, a shadow isn't the real thing, so what could be important about it? Then I noticed a couple of verses in the Bible that use the word "shadow."

> *"He who dwells in the shelter of the Most High will rest in the shadow of the Almighty." (Psalm 91:1)*

> *"I have put my words in your mouth and covered you with the shadow of my hand." (Isaiah 51:16)*

I pondered what it means to be under the shadow of God's hand or resting in the shadow of the Almighty. I realized that a shadow can't exist without the real thing or the real person nearby. A shadow is a copy, a replica, the same shape as the person. In fact, a shadow can't be separated from what is casting it or what it represents. Now I understand that a shadow is very powerful. The shadow is proof of the reality that is not far away.

FORESHADOWS OF THE LORD

Throughout the Old Testament there are foreshadows or

types or pictures of the Lord Jesus. Whereas a shadow is a shape or image of something, a foreshadow adds the dimension of prediction or foretelling to the meaning. A foreshadow gives hints about something or someone to come in the future. It may be a sign or a symbol that helps us to know what the person or event will be like.

The foreshadows of Jesus in the Old Testament are people or events that paint a picture that gives us a greater understanding of Jesus. Some are very clear pictures and some are discovered the more we read and study Scriptures. Here are some foreshadows of Jesus found in the Old Testament:

JESUS THE LAMB OF GOD

As early as Genesis chapter 3, we read of the foreshadowing of Jesus' sacrifice for our sins when God shed the blood of an innocent animal to make a covering for Adam and Eve after they sinned. In Exodus 12:7, Jesus is foreshadowed as the Jews were required to kill a perfect lamb whose blood would spare them from the judgment God brought upon Egypt. Jesus is also foreshadowed in the Mosaic Law which required the sacrifice of innocent, spotless animals for the forgiveness and atonement of the sins of the people.

JESUS OUR SUBSTITUTE

One of the clearest pictures or images of the substitutionary death of Jesus is in Genesis 22. God tested Abraham by commanding him to sacrifice his son, Isaac, as a burnt offering to the Lord. When Abraham obeyed and was about to kill his son, the Lord stopped him and provided a ram instead for Abraham to offer as a sacrifice. He told Abraham to exchange the ram for Isaac. The ram was sacrificed and Isaac's life was spared. This is what Jesus did for us, He is our substitute! He endured the punishment that we deserve by shedding His own blood on the cross.

JESUS OUR REDEEMER

The foreshadowing of Jesus as our Redeemer is pictured in the lives of Joseph and Boaz in the Old Testament. Joseph was the redeemer of the entire nation of Israel, saving them from death by famine (Genesis 37-50). In the book of Ruth, Boaz paid the price of redemption, paying the debt owed, buying the land, and taking Ruth as his wife. Boaz became her redeemer, a beautiful picture and foreshadow of what Christ would eventually do for us by paying the price to redeem us.

JESUS ON THE CROSS

Numbers 21:6-9 describes an event that foreshadows Jesus being lifted up on the cross. When the people were dying from venomous snakes in the wilderness, God instructed Moses to create a bronze snake and place it on a pole. Anyone who was bitten by a snake and looked up at the bronze snake would live. It sounds like a strange story, but this solution required that the people lift their eyes up and out of their circumstances and trust the Lord. This event foreshadowed the Lord Jesus being lifted up on the cross. Jesus said in John 3:14-15;

> *"Just as Moses lifted up the snake in the desert, so the Son of Man must be lifted up, that everyone who believes in him may have eternal life."*

PART 4: THE STAR OF THE BIBLE

THE GIFT OF SHADOWS

The pictures, types, and foreshadows of Jesus in the Old Testament are proof of the authority and truth of the Scriptures. How could Moses or Joseph or Boaz have possibly known that events in their lives would serve as pictures of their Savior to come? These shadows are evidence of Jesus and the framework of history and "His" story in the Scriptures. They are gleaming threads of clues and affirmations of the Messiah in the tapestry of the Bible.

CHAPTER 27

Everlasting Jesus

Everlasting. Think about that word. Eternal, forever, no beginning, no end. You can't even think of everlasting as a long, long time because it is not governed or constrained by time. Time is the measurement between events, an interval, a period of duration. Everlasting is not measured by time. Everlasting is... forever.

We live in the physical world that God created. We experience beginnings, endings, and growth or change in between. But there is so much more that extends beyond what you and I can touch, see, and comprehend within the physical universe. The world has boundaries and humans have limited lifespans. Yet we know there's more. After all, the Bible tells us that God has "set eternity in the hearts of men." (Ecclesiastes 3:11)

And it's true, people have always known inherently that there is more to life than what we see. When people die, there is an afterlife. And life after death is forever. We just know that we know.

Why? Because God put eternity in our hearts, even though we don't understand it and are unable to explain it. Nevertheless, we long for it, we think about it, and we believe there is such a thing as... forever.

Jesus brought "forever" to the forefront of people's minds when He said, "Before Abraham was born, I am!" (John 8:58b) Immediately the religious leaders who were questioning Jesus picked up stones to try to kill Him.

Why were the religious leaders so incensed? Because "I am" is the term God used to identify Himself when speaking to Moses at the burning bush in Exodus 3:14. "I am" refers to God Himself, the eternal God who has no beginning and no end. The Pharisees recognized that Jesus was claiming to be God, which they considered blasphemy. They also attempted to stone Jesus another time saying, "… because you, a mere man, claim to be God." (John 10:33) This claim ultimately led to Jesus' crucifixion. The religious leaders insisted that Pilate crucify Jesus saying,

> *"We have a law, and according to that law he must die, because he claimed to be the Son of God."*
> *(John 19:7)*

IS JESUS THE ETERNAL GOD?

When people claim that Jesus was a prophet or a good teacher, but that He isn't God, they should consider these questions:

- ✛ If Jesus was a good teacher, why did He claim to be God?
- ✛ If Jesus was a prophet, did He say things that were untrue?
- ✛ If Jesus made claims about Himself that were not true, wouldn't that make Him a liar?

The fact is, Jesus' bold claims about Himself do not leave room for a range of beliefs about Him. He is either God in human flesh or He's not. It's one or the other. The claim that

Jesus was simply a prophet or a wise teacher or a man who represented God is not a viable statement. Such a claim would be inaccurate because a prophet, a good man, or a good teacher would not lie.

For a proper understanding of who Jesus really is, we turn to Scripture. The Bible teaches that Jesus is:

✛ *Everlasting Father*

> *"And he will be called Wonderful Counselor, Mighty God, Everlasting Father, Prince of Peace."*
> *(Isaiah 9:6b)*

✛ *Creator*

> *"Through him all things were made; without him nothing was made that has been made." (John 1:3)*

✛ *God*

> *"I and the Father are one." (John 10:30)*

✛ *Messiah*

> *"Again the high priest asked him, 'Are you the Christ, the Son of the Blessed One?' 'I am,' said Jesus. 'And you will see the Son of Man sitting at the right hand of the Mighty One and coming on the clouds of heaven.'" (Mark 14:61b-62)*

✛ *Savior*

> *"And we have seen and testify that the Father has sent his Son to be the Savior of the world."*
> *(1 John 4:14)*

ETERNAL QUALITIES OF JESUS

Notice that the descriptive words such as "God,"

"Creator," and "Everlasting Father" have eternal qualities. Because Jesus was a man who ate fish around a campfire with his Disciples, it is hard to comprehend that He is the eternal Lord. We think of Jesus as being limited, as human beings are. And in a way, Jesus did "limit" Himself by clothing Himself in flesh. He did not come to earth in His full glory. He lived as a humble servant. He was fully man and fully God. He lived as a man in real human flesh, yet performed miracles as only God can do. He healed people, He calmed the stormy seas, He gave sight to the blind, and He raised the dead. Finally, He walked out of the grave after being crucified!

Those who walked with Him saw the human side of Jesus, with glimpses of His eternal qualities. One day we will see the fullness of Jesus, in His glory, rather than in His temporary human flesh. Therefore, we should not allow our belief and understanding of Jesus to be constrained by the humanity of Jesus.

FOREVER VS. EVERLASTING

You and I will live forever… somewhere. We will live either in Heaven with the Lord or in Hell with Satan, demons, and all those who rejected Jesus' provision of salvation. "Forever" means having no end. We each have a beginning, the day we were conceived. Then, the day we were born we began life on earth. We have a soul that will never die. We will live forever.

Forever is different from everlasting. Forever has a beginning and no end. Everlasting has no beginning and no end. Jesus is everlasting. Jesus is God. Jesus has no beginning and no end.

CHAPTER 28

The Feasts Fulfilled

If you've studied the Old Testament, you may have been impressed by the feasts that God's people celebrated throughout the year. Their feasts were not like our dinner parties of today. We have a celebration for a few hours, but in ancient times, the Jewish people celebrated feasts for days, some lasted seven days. Their feasts were long celebrations, commemorations, and reminders of specific important events.

The Old Testament provides physical examples of spiritual truths and realities, many of which were to be fulfilled in the future. In some cases, the specific purpose of the feast was to celebrate a reality that took place but would also take place again in the future. The fulfillment of the feast would be manifested in the person of Jesus.

God instructed His people to celebrate seven feasts, and each one carries special significance. Learning about the feasts helps us to have a greater and deeper understanding of Jesus. Here are short overviews of several of the feasts that God instructed the Israelites to honor and celebrate. As you read, notice how the festivals point to Jesus in a special way.

Passover: (Lev. 23:4-8) The word "Passover" comes from the events of the night that the Israelites were freed from oppression and slavery in Egypt. Pharoah had refused to free the Jewish people from bondage and God sent ten plagues to Egypt as judgment. Pharoah continued to refuse God's command to "let my people go!" This night was the final plague, the final judgment that would force Pharoah to release God's people. The Jews were instructed to kill a lamb and apply the blood on the doorframe of their homes. The blood would save them as the angel of death "passed over" their homes during the plague of the death of the firstborn in Egypt.

This feast is one of the most powerful pictures of Jesus, our spotless lamb whose blood was shed for our sins. Jesus was crucified on the day the lambs were being killed for Passover. *The Lamb of God was crucified on Passover.* The feast of Passover that began at the time of the exodus was fulfilled by Jesus on the day of His crucifixion.

Feast of Trumpets and Day of Atonement: (Lev. 23:23-32) The Feast of Trumpets (Rosh Hashana) is a celebration of the Jewish New Year and is a time of preparation for Yom Kippur, the Day of Atonement. The people fast and spend time in confession and repentance, preparing for the most holy day of the year, Yom Kippur. In the Old Testament, on the Day of Atonement, the High Priest would enter the Holy of Holies in the Temple and present a sacrifice for the atonement of the sins of the nation of Israel.

Jesus fulfilled the Day of Atonement by shedding His blood on the cross. Instead of the blood of an animal, Jesus shed His own blood. 1 John 2:2 tells us that He atoned for the "sins of the world." The Day of Atonement among the Jewish people took place once a year, whereas Jesus' atonement for sin is *once and for all.*

Feast of Tabernacles: (Lev. 23:33-35) This feast celebrates God's protection when the Israelites wandered in the wilderness for 40 years. The Israelites lived in tents and temporary structures while they were in the desert. God Himself dwelled among them in a temporary tent, which was a temple called the tabernacle. God "tabernacled" with His people.

Jesus fulfilled this feast by being called "Immanuel" which means "God with us." (Matthew 1:23) He was clothed in human flesh, a temporary tabernacle, to dwell with man and walk among men on earth. John 1:14 tells us, "The Word became flesh and made his dwelling among us."

Jesus fulfills this feast spiritually because He tabernacles with Believers by indwelling them through the Holy Spirit. (John 14:23) He will also fulfill this feast physically when He returns to earth as described in the Book of Revelation. He will tabernacle again with men by ruling from Jerusalem for 1,000 years. (Revelation 20:4-6)

Each of the seven prescribed feasts of the Hebrew people has special meaning. The Old Testament painted pictures, using symbols and visual significance so that Jesus would be recognized. The feasts and symbols weave together to *prove* that Jesus is the fulfillment.

CHAPTER 29

Why Did Jesus Come to Earth?

The Bible teaches that Jesus came to give His life, shed His blood, and atone for the sins of the world. This clear and concise answer is found in John 3:16-17:

> *"For God so loved the world that he gave his one and only Son, that whoever believes in him shall not perish but have eternal life. For God did not send his Son into the world to condemn the world, but to save the world through him."*

Jesus suffered and died on the cross as payment for the sins of the world. Our sins were put on Him and He endured the wrath of God, the punishment that was due to us. He took on our sins and gave us His righteousness, yes… His righteousness, so that we would not be condemned for our sin and perish in Hell but live eternally in Heaven. This act of the exchange of sin for righteousness is called "The Great Exchange" in Christianity.

> *"God made him who had no sin to be sin for us, so that in him we might become the righteousness of God." (2 Corinthians 5:21)*

A great thing was accomplished on the cross! Our sin was

placed on Jesus and His robe of righteousness is placed on those who believe and have faith in Him. Simply stated, Jesus exchanged His righteousness for our sin and we as Believers exchanged our sin for His righteousness. The Great Exchange.

That is the answer to the question of why Jesus came to earth. It was His love for all of humanity. His mission was to sacrifice His life to provide atonement for sin, reverse the curse that began in the Garden of Eden, and provide salvation to all who would come to believe in Him.

Although accomplishing the work of salvation was Jesus' primary mission while on earth, He also accomplished many other things. Here are other important results of Jesus' life on earth:

JESUS REVEALED THE KINGDOM OF GOD

Jesus said that the time "has come" and the kingdom of God "is near." (Mark 1:15) What is the Kingdom of God? A kingdom is the realm where a king rules and reigns. When asked by the Pharisees about the Kingdom of God, Jesus answered by saying, "...the kingdom of God is within you." (Luke 17:21) Some versions of the Bible say, "among you" or "in your midst." Jesus was explaining that the Kingdom of God is not a physical, earthly empire, rather the place where God rules and reigns is in the hearts of those who believe.

Christians understand this because, upon receiving the gift of the Holy Spirit, we now have the Kingdom of God within us. No longer are we on the throne of our lives, but someone else rules: Jesus is our King and reigns over our hearts and lives.

Why Did Jesus Come to Earth?

Jesus' Life on Earth Changed the World

We may not be fully aware of all the things we enjoy in this world that are a direct result of the life and ministry of Jesus Christ. Jesus' impact goes much further than faith and religious beliefs. Many universities in our country and around the world began with the foundation of Christianity. The schools in America began with the intent to teach children to read the Bible.

The calendar used by most of the world is based on the birth of Jesus Christ. It is quite extraordinary to consider that most of the world throughout the centuries has measured days and years by the birth and death of Jesus.

Jesus broke new ground by the way He treated women. In Jesus' day women were treated as inferior and had no rights. Even their testimony in court wasn't considered valid. Yet the first person to whom Jesus revealed that He was the Messiah was a woman. The first person He appeared to after His resurrection was a woman. And those women testified as eyewitnesses of their encounters with Jesus!

Jesus treated all people with love and dignity, regardless of economic status. He ministered to the poor and the "unclean" and set an example for the entire world to understand that all people are valued by their Creator. Each person is loved by God.

Jesus continues to impact and change the lives of those who believe in Him. His Church continues to grow, and the Bible continues to be the bestselling book of all time. All of this from a humble preacher who had no higher education, no weapons, no money, and never wrote anything down. Yet Jesus has been the most influential person in all of history!

CHAPTER 30

God Revealed Himself Through Jesus

Have you seen glimpses of God? Possibly you've experienced miracles in your own life. Maybe you've heard other people give testimony about what God has done for them. There are so many ways we see God at work in our world.

The ancient Israelites relied on prophets, Scriptures, angels, and miracles, but the Bible tells us in Hebrews 1:2 that "in these last days" God has spoken to us through his Son. The clearest picture of God is through Jesus.

This is so important. There are many ways to see God, get a glimpse of Him, learn about Him, see Him by faith, and watch Him work in this world. But the plainest and best way to see, understand, and know God is through His Son, Jesus.

WHY CHRISTIANITY IS UNIQUE

Many people around the world believe in God, or a god, or their own version of God. But there is only one God. Apart from the one true God, the word "god" simply means a deity, someone or something that one believes has divine power. But when we come face to face with Jesus, God in human flesh, we now can define the one true God very specifically.

There is no cloudiness or variation or option to define God in our own way. No, Jesus defines Himself by who He is, what He says, and what He does.

Could this be why God chose this particular and clear-cut way to reveal Himself to mankind? Instead of a dictionary definition or a person's description of God, we have Jesus. He explains Himself, He displays His character, and He clearly and undeniably reveals God to us.

No room for argument! If you define your god to me and it doesn't match Jesus, then we are not in agreement. When people from other religious belief systems describe their gods, does their description line up with Jesus, who He is, and what He said? If not, then they are not talking about my God.

Some say there are many roads to God. They say that the god of other major religions is really the same as the God of the Bible. That is false. If you are faced with someone who believes this, ask the person to describe God. "Tell me about the God you believe in." Then, tell the person about the God of the Bible who revealed Himself through Jesus Christ. They will see that Jesus is not the same as their own deity.

Here's why:
- Other religions require conformity to a system of works in order to be right with God.
- Other religions believe in a god who is powerful, yet far away and not personal.
- Other religions teach that eternal life or reward in the afterlife is dependent on you, your good works, and your actions. In other words, you *earn* your reward of eternal life.

CHRISTIANITY IS DIFFERENT FROM OTHER RELIGIONS BECAUSE:

Jesus wants an individual relationship with every person who believes in Him.

Jesus sacrificed His life, shedding His own blood as payment for our sins.

Salvation is by grace alone, through Christ and His finished work on the cross. We are saved by grace, not our own works.

Jesus grants salvation to those who have faith and believe in Him. Salvation is a free gift to those who accept it and receive it by faith.

Jesus sends the Holy Spirit to permanently indwell Believers.

Good works are the fruit of salvation, the result of the Holy Spirit working in and through us. Good works are not the way to earn or be deserving of eternal life in Heaven. If we could do it on our own, why do we need a Savior?

There is no other message in any other religion like the Gospel message of salvation by the grace of Jesus, who was crucified and resurrected from the grave. Jesus is not like any other god of any other religious system around the world.

In fact, if Jesus is God, then all other world religions are false. John 14:6 says,

> *"Jesus answered, 'I am the way and the truth and the life. No one comes to the Father except through me.'"*

Only one way? Jesus leaves no option for other roads to the Father. Our choice is either to accept or reject Jesus and His offer of salvation and reconciliation with God. Jesus said in John 15:23,

> *"He who hates me hates my Father as well."*

Rejection of Jesus is rejection of God the Father.

But many prefer their own version of God! When Jesus preached and performed miracles during His earthly ministry, people loved to listen to Him and experience the miracles. They followed Him when He healed people and fed thousands from a few fish and loaves of bread. But when His teachings were hard, many followers abandoned Him. They didn't like what Jesus was saying. At times, they didn't agree with His teachings and wanted to continue living in their own way.

When this happened, Jesus turned to the twelve Disciples and asked them if they also wanted to leave Him. John 6:68-69 says,

> *"Simon Peter answered him, 'Lord, to whom shall we go? You have the words of eternal life. We believe and know that you are the Holy One of God.'"*

Peter recognized that there was no other option. Jesus is God. There is nowhere else to go for eternal life. Will we believe? Will we follow Jesus? When faced with Jesus, this is the choice that we all must make. *There is no other option.*

This is the decision that is presented to us through the Gospel message. If we want to know God, we must seek to know Jesus. If we know Jesus, then we know the Father. Jesus said in John 14:9,

> *"Anyone who has seen me has seen the Father...."*

Jesus also plainly stated,

> *"I and the Father are one." (John 10:30)*

When we finally believe and understand that Jesus is God, not a lesser version of God, but God in human flesh, we will worship Him.

THE SUPREMACY OF JESUS

Though it may be hard to understand, our God is a triune God. Our God is one yet exists in three distinct persons. This is what the Bible teaches and is a core doctrine of Christianity. The Father, Son, and Holy Spirit are equal. This Christian doctrine is worthy of much study to grasp its depth and significance.

Jesus plainly spoke of the Trinity when He said,

> *"Therefore go and make disciples of all nations, baptizing them in the name of the Father and of the Son and of the Holy Spirit." (Matthew 28:19)*

Colossians 1:15-20 is very thorough in explaining the supremacy of Jesus:

> *"He is the image of the invisible God, the firstborn over all creation. For by him all things were created: things in heaven and on earth, visible and invisible, whether thrones or powers or rulers or authorities; all things have been created by him and for him. He is before all things, and in him all things hold together. And he is the head of the body, the church; he is the beginning and the firstborn from among the dead, so that in everything he might have the supremacy. For God was pleased to have all his fullness dwell in him, and through him to reconcile to himself all things, whether things on earth or things in heaven, by making peace through his blood, shed on the cross."*

The Colossians passage covers why Jesus is so important

when we consider our Christian faith. Here are the main points of the passage:

- *Jesus is the Creator* – All things were created by Him. (vs. 16)
- *Jesus is the head of the Church* – As Christians, we are part of the body of Christ, which is His Church. (vs. 18)
- *Jesus is the firstborn among the dead* – Because Jesus rose from the dead, Believers will follow Him in the resurrection. (vs. 18)
- *Jesus is God* – The fullness of God dwells in Jesus. (vs. 19)
- *We are reconciled to God through Jesus* – Our salvation comes from Jesus' sacrifice on the cross; He shed His blood so that we can be reconciled to God. (vs. 20)

Everything, everything, *everything* that we need to be forgiven and receive eternal life is found in Jesus. There is no other option given to us to be right with God. The bottom line is, there is no avoiding Jesus! Some claim to believe in the God of the universe, but they ignore Jesus, in whom our salvation is given.

Jesus has all authority in heaven and on earth.

> *"Then Jesus came to them and said, 'All authority in heaven and on earth has been given to me.'"*
> *(Matthew 28:18)*

It may be hard to grasp Jesus' equality to God because of his meekness and submissiveness to the Father. Jesus submitted to God and lived a sinless, obedient life because He chose to submit to God the Father. His submission relates to His role, not His essence. Submission to the Father does not mean that Jesus is inferior to the Father. Hebrews 10:7 says,

> *"Then I said, 'Here I am—it is written about me in the scroll—I have come to do your will, my God.'"*

ALL JUDGMENT BELONGS TO JESUS

God has given judgment of all things to Jesus. John 5:22 tells us:

> *"Moreover, the Father judges no one, but has entrusted all judgment to the Son."*

The Bible teaches that there are two types of judgment. One is for Christians and the other for the "wicked."

Christians are saved and sealed for eternity. Judgment will not change the salvation of saints. As Christians, we will give an accounting of what we did with what was entrusted to us. Jesus explained this in a parable found in Luke 19:11-26. Christians will stand before the Lord to give an account.

Revelation 20:11-15 describes what is referred to as the Great White Throne of Judgment. This judgment is generally understood to be for unbelievers. The passage tells us that anyone whose name is not in the Book of Life will be cast into the Lake of Fire.

As Christians, we seek to serve the Lord as good stewards of what He has entrusted to us. We long to hear the words of the master in the parable of Matthew 25:14-30. He said in verse 21,

> *"Well done, good and faithful servant!"*

GOD'S PLAN IS MANIFESTED THROUGH JESUS

We have learned from the Bible that Jesus is the central

figure throughout Scripture. The Messiah. The Everlasting Father. The King of Kings. Lord of Lords. Everything will come to fulfillment through Jesus, as prophesied in the book of Revelation.

Jesus has done exactly what He said when He left the earth. He has built His Church and nothing has been able to stand against it. Matthew 16:18 says,

> *"...and on this rock I will build my church, and the gates of Hades will not overcome it."*

What is the rock that Jesus said would be the foundation, the rock upon which He would build His Church? It is the statement that Peter said after Jesus asked him, "Who do you say that I am?" Peter answered in Matthew 16:16,

> *"You are the Christ, the Son of the living God."*

OUR PERSONAL RELATIONSHIP WITH GOD IS THROUGH JESUS

Jesus is our intercessor, our advocate, our mediator. The book of Hebrews teaches us that Jesus is our High Priest. The role of the High Priest in the temple was to intercede for the Jewish people. Only the High Priest could go beyond the veil into the Holy of Holies to pray for forgiveness on behalf of the people.

Jesus is our mediator, our High Priest. When Jesus died on the cross He proclaimed, "It is finished." What was finished? The work of atonement, in other words, payment for the sins of the world. Luke 23:45 tells us that the moment of Jesus' death, the veil of the temple was torn in two, the curtain that separated people from the presence of God in the Holy of Holies. The physical tearing of the veil in the temple signified that Jesus' death opened the way into the presence of God. Now we can approach the throne of God on the basis of our faith in Jesus.

Through Jesus we now can enter into God's presence... forgiven and cleansed!

RESURRECTION DAY – PROPHECY FULFILLED

The Disciples were not expecting His resurrection, even though Jesus had told them that He would be killed and would rise again in three days. (Matthew 20:17-19) When Jesus died on the cross, the Romans pierced His side to confirm that He was dead. His body was buried in a tomb, with a huge stone placed over the entrance. The tomb entrance was sealed with the official Roman seal. Roman guards were posted at the tomb to prevent anyone from stealing the body.

Just as Jesus said, He rose from the dead on the third day after His death. What a day that was for the followers of Jesus! Our Lord was raised from the dead, and we still celebrate His resurrection every year. Believers will follow Him in His resurrection and live with Him forever in Heaven.

Do you remember the prophecy that God spoke in Genesis 3:15?

> *"... he will crush your head and you will strike his heel."*

This prophecy was fulfilled with Jesus' crucifixion and resurrection. Jesus was victorious over Satan's ultimate weapon against us... death!

> *"And having disarmed the powers and authorities, he made a public spectacle of them, triumphing over them by the cross." (Colossians 2:15)*

CHAPTER 31

The Revelation of Jesus Christ

If the testimonies in the Gospels are not enough to convince people that Jesus is the One True God, we finally come to the book of Revelation.

Revelation is a book of prophecy concerning what is to come and what will take place at the end times of this world. And finally, finally, finally, Jesus is coming again (as He promised), in full glory, to place His feet anew on this earth! He will not come as He did the first time, allowing men to spit on Him, flog Him, and pound nails into His hands and feet. No, this time He will come in His full glory and power to redeem His Church, judge the earth, defeat Satan, and destroy evil once and for all. He will come in full radiant glory as King and Victor and Lord. He will come in triumph on a white horse, with many crowns on His head and this written on His robe and thigh: King of Kings and Lord of Lords. (Revelation 19:11-16) At that time Jesus will fight and win the battle of Armageddon, which is the fight against Satan and evil. Jesus will establish His Kingdom on earth and rule from Jerusalem for 1,000 years. (Revelation 19:19-20 and 20:4-6).

PART 4: THE STAR OF THE BIBLE

A GLIMPSE OF HIS GLORY

When Jesus lived on earth, He appeared in glory to three of His Disciples. Jesus revealed his glory to Peter, James, and John, His most intimate Disciples, to strengthen their faith. They went up a mountain to pray, but then Jesus was transfigured and shone bright as the sun, and his garments became white as light. (Matthew 17:2) Moses and Elijah appeared there also and talked with Jesus. Then, a bright cloud covered them and God spoke from the cloud and said,

> *"This is my Son, whom I love; with him I am well pleased. Listen to him!" (Matthew 17:5)*

Jesus gave Peter, James, and John an unforgettable glimpse of His glory to reassure them as the time of His crucifixion was approaching. They saw Jesus in His glory and heard the voice of God confirming the Lordship of Jesus.

Wouldn't it be wonderful if we also could have a glimpse of Jesus' glory? Something that confirms our hope? Something that proves that Jesus really is who He claimed to be?

We are given more than a glimpse of Jesus in the book of Revelation. We have a descriptive picture and narrative of what is to come. For those who will take the time and make the effort to study Revelation, they will be blessed with inside knowledge, learning the secrets and the truth about events that are going to come to pass. John wrote the book of Revelation and said in 1:3,

> *"Blessed is the one who reads aloud the words of this prophecy, and blessed are those who hear it and take to heart what is written in it, because the time is near."*

The Revelation of Jesus Christ

For more than a glimpse of His glory, a thorough understanding of Revelation will leave us in awe of the King of Kings, the Savior of the world.

THE STAR OF REVELATION

John, one of the closest Disciples to Jesus, was the one to receive the visions and revelations that are in the book of Revelation. John says in the first sentence of the book, "the revelation of Jesus Christ." (Revelation 1:1) John is testifying to everything he saw, the Word of God, and the testimony of Jesus Christ. (Revelation 1:2)

Because of the complexities of Revelation, not all pastors and theologians agree on certain points. Despite differences in interpretation, we can study and gain a good understanding of what the book holds for us. I encourage you to read Revelation and you might be surprised that there is much that you will understand. This is exciting and encouraging.

Jesus instructed John to write letters to seven churches in a province of Asia. Those letters are in the book of Revelation. The letters were dictated by Jesus to each of the churches and reveal the mind of Christ concerning issues and practices of the churches. He speaks stern warnings as well as some commendations. Oh, to know the mind of Christ! And we have His thoughts right in the book of Revelation.

Further in Revelation we learn from the visions that John described. Much of this is written in symbolism. One must really understand the symbolism of the Old Testament to be able to correlate some of the intended meanings. Why was so much of Revelation written in symbols? One of the reasons is that the casual reader will simply not understand and isn't even meant to understand the deep messages from God to His people. But Revelation will be understood by those who love the Lord and seek to learn. So it is a mystery to those who don't know Christ, and a revelation to those who do know Christ.

The other important reason this book is written in symbolic language is that visions are hard to describe in words. I believe that some of the events and things that John saw are things that have not been invented yet! For example, if the fires described in Revelation are the result of nuclear weapons, John would not have had the knowledge to specifically describe such an event. Or if the flying locusts that torment and kill humans are drones of our modern day, there would have been no words to specifically describe them.

Though some symbolic language is a challenge for us to study and understand, some prophecies are written in plain language and we accept it just as it is written. For example, when Jesus ascended into the cloud, an angel appeared to the disciples who were standing there looking up at the sky. The angel said,

> *"This same Jesus who has been taken from you into heaven, will come back in the same way you have seen him go into heaven." (Acts 1:11b)*

That's a statement that we all can understand. Jesus is coming back in the same way He left, from the sky. Revelation 1:7 says this,

> *"Look, he is coming with the clouds, and every eye will see him, even those who pierced him; and all peoples on earth will mourn because of him. So shall it be! Amen."*

Those are statements of reality; no need to worry about

deciphering symbolism in those sentences!

JESUS IS COMING BACK

Before Jesus was crucified, He told His disciples plainly,

> *"The Son of Man is going to be betrayed into the hands of men. They will kill him, and on the third day he will be raised to life." (Matthew 17:22b-23a)*

Jesus told them exactly what would happen, that He would be killed, but that three days later He would rise again.

Now we have the next promise, prediction, and prophecy. We are told that Jesus will return, He is coming back to earth! We should take this very seriously as Jesus was right the first time, when He predicted His own death and resurrection.

Jesus said He will return and the Scriptures explain His promise. Although there may be disagreement on the specifics, many pastors and Bible scholars agree that the Bible teaches that Jesus will first come to rapture His Church from this earth. In an instant, He will return and Believers will be caught up in the air with Christ. 1 Thessalonians 4:16-17 tells us,

> *"For the Lord himself will come down from heaven, with a loud command, with the voice of the archangel and with the trumpet call of God, and the dead in Christ will rise first. After that, we who are still alive and are left will be caught up together with them in the clouds to meet the Lord in the air. And so we will be with the Lord forever."*

Then, Jesus will come back as described in Revelation chapters 19 and 20. Jesus will return as King of Kings, Lord of Lords. He will fight and defeat "the beast and the kings of the earth and their armies" as described in Revelation 19:19-21. Chapter 20:1-4 tells us that Satan will be bound for 1,000 years and Jesus will reign on earth for 1,000 years. After that, Satan will be released once more and will deceive the nations. But Jesus will conquer Satan who will be "thrown into the lake of burning sulfur" as described in Revelation 20:7-10.

Jesus will do what He promised, He is coming back, He will take His church (the Believers) out of this world, and He will return to fight and have victory over Satan and evil once and for all. Knowing this, we should be wise, which means to be ready. We should make sure that we are prepared and not lazy regarding our commitment to the Lord Jesus. We have much to do if we want to be fruitful in furthering His Kingdom on earth before He returns!

Since we don't know exactly when Jesus will return, we must be ready at all times.

> *"Therefore, keep watch, because you do not know on what day your Lord will come." (Matthew 24:42)*

WHY READ REVELATION?

For years I really didn't pay too much attention to the book of Revelation. I felt that it really didn't pertain to my everyday life and thought I would not understand it. I knew the book was about the end times and Jesus' second coming, and I just settled it in my mind, *Whatever Jesus does is fine with me. I don't need to learn about it!* Although I had heard sermons about the letters to the churches and about some of the future events, I wasn't motivated to do any personal study of Revelation.

Years later, I began to delve into the study of Revelation. Wow! I learned how important it is to understand what God has planned for people and this world. After all, I love Jesus more than anything, why wouldn't I be interested in His plan to return to this earth? This is a big deal! Jesus is coming back, and when He does, He will put an end to sin, suffering, pain, and sickness. Not only that, He has a plan to end the influence and power of Satan and his demons forever. Imagine a world without Satan tempting and leading people to do evil!

The book of Revelation gives us hope in our everyday lives. We know that our trials and the pain and the confusion of this current world are temporary. It's a battle, but we already know who is going to win. We know the end of the story. We know that God has a plan. We know that God is really in control, that sinful man can't go beyond what God allows in order to fulfill His ultimate plan of victory.

Reading and understanding God's plan not only gives us confidence, faith, and hope in our God, but it provides a purpose for us. Our purpose is to further God's Kingdom while we have a chance, while we are alive, while Jesus tarries before His return. In fact, the reason Jesus hasn't returned yet is because of His great love for us:

> *"The Lord is not slow in keeping his promise, as some understand slowness. He is patient with you, not wanting anyone to perish, but everyone to come to repentance." (2 Peter 3:9)*

GOD'S FAITHFULNESS TO ISRAEL, HIS CHOSEN PEOPLE

God has been faithful to His chosen people and will continue to display His hesed love for them. Revelation tells us that Jesus will set foot in Jerusalem again. The Messiah is going to return! And there will come a time when God's chosen people will recognize their Messiah and believe in Him.

PART 4: THE STAR OF THE BIBLE

Romans 11:26-27 tells us:

> *"...and so all Israel will be saved, as it is written: 'The deliverer will come from Zion; he will turn godlessness away from Jacob. And this is my covenant with them when I take away their sins.'"*

JESUS IN HIS FULL GLORY

If you ever doubt or lack faith or live in disbelief, or wonder if Jesus really is who He says He is, the book of Revelation will strengthen your spirit. Revelation is about Jesus. The King, the Powerful, the Almighty, the Lord of all, and the Victor over evil.

A picture of Jesus appeared in the beginning of the Bible, in Genesis 3, all the way through the entire Bible, culminating in the book of Revelation.

He is the Star of the Bible!

CONCLUSION

The last verse of the Bible is Revelation 22:21,

> *"The grace of the Lord Jesus be with God's people. Amen."*

This final verse is a blessing, a benediction, a prayer for the grace of the Lord Jesus to be with God's people.

Think back to the very first verse of the Bible.

> *"In the beginning God created the heavens and the earth."*

The first verse introduced us to God the Creator of the heavens and the earth. All the pages in the books after the first verse reveal who this Almighty God is, what He does, and His plans for His people. Then we reach the last and final verse of the Bible.

The conclusion of a book is very important. It should remind the reader of the point of the book. It should be a recap of the purpose of the book. John's final sentence reminds us, in a powerful way, three important purposes of the Bible:

GOD'S GRACE

If you have ever read the Bible from start to finish, you will have read the following:

+ The history of the Jewish nation

- God's relationship with His chosen people
- God's Law and standards for living life
- Prophecies about the coming of the Messiah
- True life stories of individual people
- Foreshadows, pictures, and symbols of Jesus
- Songs of praise and wisdom for life
- Eyewitness accounts of the birth, life, death, and resurrection of our Savior, the Lord Jesus Christ
- How the church developed and grew
- Letters to the churches containing Christian doctrine and instruction
- The revelation of what is to come

Wow—that's a lot of powerful information packed into one book! One thing you should conclude at the end of your journey through the Bible is that God is love and the grace He pours out on people, nations, and the world is *immense.*

If you can imagine a world without the grace of God, it would probably be a place similar to Hell itself. Imagine a world where the sun doesn't shine and rain does not fall. Imagine a disorderly world around us, nature not following the natural law that God designed. Nature unleashing its fury. No beauty, no color, only darkness.

We may not fully comprehend just how involved God really is in the running and sustaining of the world. He is everywhere; He is keeping the beauty and orderliness of nature and the earthly systems running as they should. When you think of the colorful beauty of flowers that just seem to pop up on their own around the countryside, what could be more beautiful?

We have a marvelous opportunity to live in His grace for a temporary time, until we leave this earth or until Jesus returns.

JESUS CHRIST

When John reminds us of grace, he says it is the grace of the Lord Jesus. It is through Jesus that we are reconciled to God the Father. Jesus is everything to us. He is the exact representation of God the Father. All things are manifested through Jesus.

> *"The Son is the radiance of God's glory and the exact representation of his being, sustaining all things by his powerful word." (Hebrews 1:3a)*

God has chosen to manifest our salvation through Jesus. Not only that, but our lives, our hope, our victory, our sanctification, and our eternal life are established through Jesus. This is how God relates to the masterpiece of His creation… through His Son, Jesus Christ.

GOD'S PEOPLE

All Believers are God's people. And those who are not yet Believers are invited to believe. It's all about God's love for His people. He has had so much patience and grace throughout centuries of enduring man's rebellion against Him. God's hesed love is stubborn, faithful, and persistent.

AMEN.

Now it's time to look at the very last word of the Bible. **Amen.** This is actually a wonderful word of response that you and I use all the time. At the end of our prayers we say, "amen." We hear something we agree with and we respond, "amen." Some of us even respond loudly and enthusiastically to a great sermon, "AMEN!"

What are we actually saying? We are saying, "it is true" or "so be it" or let it be." It is agreement and confirmation of something that has been stated. The meaning comes from a Hebrew word that means "firm" or "fixed." It is also related to a Hebrew verb that means "to be reliable or trusted."[7]

That means that "amen" is a very important word. Especially if you agree with something, want to confirm it, or desire for something to come to pass just as the words were spoken. *May it be Lord, just as You have said, let it come to pass!* When we say "amen" to God, we are in agreement with Him, submitting to His will and also asking for His words to be manifested.

What a perfect word to end the entire revelation of God, the Holy Scriptures, the Bible that you and I read. We agree that God's Word is reliable, trustworthy, and perfect. *It is true. So be it. Let your will be done.*

AMEN!

> *"Jesus did many other miraculous signs in the presence of his disciples, which are not recorded in this book. But these are written that you may believe that Jesus is the Christ, the Son of God, and that by believing you may have life in his name."*
> *(John 20:30-31)*

AUTHOR'S NOTE – WHAT'S NEXT?

Best Seller was written to encourage those who have never read the Bible to begin reading the Word of God. My desire is that you don't miss out on this magnificent gift that God has given to us! For those who do read the Bible, I pray that *Best Seller* has increased your knowledge and strengthened your belief in the trustworthiness of the Scriptures.

I have also woven in gems of truth that I have learned over 40 years of Bible study. I continue to search the Scriptures to go deeper into the revelation and the mind of God. I know from my own experience that the Bible is an unlimited treasure and I will keep digging deeper into the valuable riches of His Word.

What will you do with the treasure of the Bible? Have the pages of *Best Seller* created within you a thirst to study God's Word? Will you pursue the Lord and continue to dig for more of the priceless treasure of the Word of God?

I pray that *Best Seller* has ignited within you an eagerness to study the Bible and become equipped with facts to explain and defend the Word of God. May you confidently share this treasure, this precious and valuable message with others as you go out into an unbelieving world that needs the Lord.

STEPS TO SALVATION

> *"For God so loved the world that he gave his one and only Son, that whoever believes in Him shall not perish but have eternal life." (John 3:16)*

For those who have not yet placed their faith in Jesus, below are the steps to become a Christian.

STEPS TO SALVATION

1. Repent – Admit that you are a sinner and confess your sins to the Lord. Repent means to turn around, go in a new direction, change your mind. You must not only confess your sin, but turn from it.
2. Believe and receive – Place your faith in Jesus Christ as your Lord and Savior. Believe in His sacrifice on the cross for your sins and His resurrection from the dead. Invite Him into your heart and surrender your life to Him. When you do this, the Holy Spirit will come and permanently indwell your heart and seal you for eternity.

> *"If you confess with your mouth, 'Jesus is Lord,' and believe in your heart that God raised him from the dead, you will be saved." (Romans 10:9)*

> *"I am the resurrection and the life. He who believes in me will live, even though he dies; and whoever lives and believes in me will never die." (John 11:25)*

PRAYER OF SALVATION:

"Lord Jesus, I believe that you died on the cross for my sins and that you rose again on the third day. I repent of my sin, please forgive me and cleanse me. I choose to follow you and surrender my life to you. I receive your gift of salvation by grace. I believe that you are my Savior and my Lord. In Jesus' Name, Amen."

It is important to grow in your faith by finding a Bible-believing church and fellowshipping with other Christians. Daily study of God's Word will strengthen your faith and teach you about your Lord and Savior.

BIBLIOGRAPHY

[1] Merriam-Webster Dictionary online
   Definition of Canon
   https://www.merriam-webster.com/dictionary/canon#:~:text=4-,a,criterion%20or%20standard%20of%20judgment

[2] Storyofthebible.com
   Article: Meticulous Jewish Scribes
   https://www.storyofbible.com/meticulous-jewish-scribes.html

[3] Encyclopedia Britannica, Inc. c 2024
   Britannica, The Editors of Encyclopaedia. "Belshazzar". Encyclopedia Britannica, 16 Feb. 2024, https://www.britannica.com/biography/Belshazzar. Accessed 9 May 2024.
   https://www.britannica.com/biography/Belshazzar

[4] Patternsofevidence.com
   Article: A Brief History of Bible Translation – From Greek to English
   https://www.patternsofevidence.com/2023/02/10/a-brief-history-of-bible-translation-from-greek-to-english/#:~:text=Translation%20from%20Greek%20into%2

BIBLIOGRAPHY

0other,the%20language%20spoken%20in%20Damascus.

[5] Samford University online
Tyndale's Will to 'One Thing' resulted in English Bible (Posted by Mary Wimberley on 2009-10-30)
https://www.samford.edu/news/2009/Tyndales-Will-to-One-Thing-Resulted-in-English-Bible#:~:text=Tyndale's%20last%20words%20before%20being,every%20parish%20church%20in%20England.

[6] Patternsofevidence.com
Article: A Brief History of Bible Translation – From Greek to English
https://www.patternsofevidence.com/2023/02/10/a-brief-history-of-bible-translation-from-greek-to-english/#:~:text=Translation%20from%20Greek%20into%20other,the%20language%20spoken%20in%20Damascus.

[7] Britannica
Britannica, The Editors of Encyclopaedia. "amen". *Encyclopedia Britannica*, 3 May. 2024, https://www.britannica.com/topic/amen-prayer. Accessed 30 May 2024.

www.ingramcontent.com/pod-product-compliance
Lightning Source LLC
Chambersburg PA
CBHW022101090426
42743CB00008B/674